DANTE'S PARADISO

Borgo Press Books by S. FOWLER WRIGHT

*Arresting Delia: An Inspector Cleveland Classic Crime Novel * The Attic Murder: An Inspector Combridge & Mr. Jellipot Classic Crime Novel * The Bell Street Murders: An Inspector Combridge & Mr. Jellipot Classic Crime Novel * Beyond the Rim: A Lost Race Fantasy * Black Widow: A Classic Crime Novel * The Blue Room: A Novel of an Alternate Future * The British Colonies: No Surrender to Nazi Germany! * The Capone Caper: Mr. Jellipot vs. the King of Crime: A Classic Crime Novel * Cortéz: For God and Spain: An Historical Novel * Crime & Co.: An Inspector Cleveland Classic Crime Novel * Dante's Inferno * Dante's Paradiso * Dante's Purgatorio * David the King: An Historical Novel * Dawn: A Novel of Global Warming * Dead by Saturday: An Inspector Cleveland Classic Crime Novel * Deluge: A Novel of Global Warming * Dream; or, The Simian Maid: A Fantasy of Prehistory (Marguerite Cranleigh #1) * Elfwin: An Historical Novel of Anglo-Saxon Times * The End of the Mildew Gang: An Inspector Cauldron Classic Crime Novel (Mildew #3) * Four Callers in Razor Street: An Inspector Combridge & Mr. Jellipot Classic Crime Novel * Four Days' War: The Alternate World War II, Book Two * The Hanging of Constance Hillier: An Inspector Cleveland Classic Crime Novel * The Hidden Tribe: A Lost Race Fantasy * Inquisitive Angel: A Novel of Fantasy * The Island of Captain Sparrow: A Lost Race Fantasy * The Jordans Murder: An Inspector Combridge & Mr. Jellipot Classic Crime Novel * The King Against Anne Bickerton: A Classic Crime Novel * The Last Days of Pompeii: An Historical Novel * The Life of Sir Walter Scott: A Biography * The Lord's Right in Languedoc: An Historical Novel * Marguerite de Valois: An Historical Novel * Megiddo's Ridge: The Alternate World War II, Book Three * The Mildew Gang: An Inspector Cauldron Classic Crime Novel (Mildew #1) * Murder in Bethnal Square: An Inspector Combridge & Mr. Jellipot Classic Crime Novel * The Ordeal of Baratá: A Political Fantasy * The Police and the Public: Some Thoughts on the British System of Justice * Post-Mortem Evidence: An Inspector Combridge & Mr. Jellipot Classic Crime Novel * Power: A Political Fantasy * Prelude in Prague: The Alternate World War II, Book One * Red Ike: A Novel of Cumberland (with J. M. Denwood) * The Return of the Mildew Gang: An Inspector Cauldron Classic Crime Novel (Mildew #2) * The Rissole Mystery: An Inspector Combridge & Mr. Jellipot Classic Crime Novel * The Screaming Lake: A Lost Race Fantasy * The Secret of the Screen: An Inspector Combridge & Mr. Jellipot Classic Crime Novel * Seven Thousand in Israel: A Novel * The Siege of Malta: An Historical Novel * The Song of Songs and Other Poems * Spiders' War: A Novel of the Far Future (Marguerite Cranleigh #3) * Three Witnesses: A Classic Crime Novel * Too Much for Mr. Jellipot: An Inspector Combridge & Mr. Jellipot Classic Crime Novel * The Vengeance of Gwa: A Fantasy of Prehistory (Marguerite Cranleigh #2) * Was Murder Done? A Classic Crime Novel * Who Murdered Reynard? A Classic Crime Novel * The Wills of Jane Kanwhistle: An Inspector Combridge & Mr. Jellipot Classic Crime Novel * With Cause Enough?: An Inspector Combridge & Mr. Jellipot Classic Crime Novel * The World Below: A Novel of the Far Future * Wyndham Smith: His Adventures in the 45th Century: Science Fiction Novel*

DANTE'S PARADISO

THE DIVINE COMEDY, BOOK THREE

DANTE ALIGHIERI

Translated by S. Fowler Wright

THE BORGO PRESS
MMXII

Copyright © 2012 by the Estate of S. Fowler Wright

FIRST EDITION

Published by Wildside Press LLC

www.wildsidebooks.com

DANTE'S PARADISO

CONTENTS

PREFACE. 9
CANTO I 11
CANTO II 16
CANTO III 21
CANTO IV 26
CANTO V 31
CANTO VI 36
CANTO VII 41
CANTO VIII 46
CANTO IX 52
CANTO X 57
CANTO XI 62
CANTO XII 67
CANTO XIII 73
CANTO XIV 78
CANTO XV 83
CANTO XVI 88

CANTO XVII	94
CANTO XVIII	99
CANTO XIX	104
CANTO XX	109
CANTO XXI	114
CANTO XXII	119
CANTO XXIII	124
CANTO XXIV	128
CANTO XXV	133
CANTO XXVI	138
CANTO XXVII	143
CANTO XXVIII	148
CANTO XXIX	153
CANTO XXX	158
CANTO XXXI	163
CANTO XXXII	168
CANTO XXXIII	173
ABOUT THE AUTHOR	178

PREFACE

There are two typed unpublished manuscripts of this poem, labeled, in 1990, 'A' and 'B' for identification. This book was typed and scanned from version 'A,' and then checked against, and altered to be version 'B.' The differences are minor—and to the non-scholar—apparently academic.

Although Canto XXIII was published in *Poetry* (May 1921), *Paradiso* was never published in book form, perhaps because it did not universally reach the same standard as the other two translations. It is to be noted that the language and artistry of the original poem would in any case render it the most difficult to translate realistically.

—Gus Fowler-Wright

CANTO I

The Glory which is God, which all creates,
And all with motion quickens, penetrates
The immensities of space unequally,
In certain regions more resplendently
And less in others.
               I who write have been
In the mid-heaven of utmost light: have seen
Things which nor memory holds nor speech could tell,
Too far transcending our mortality
For human intellect to bear away.
Yet what I rescued from that holy well,
Truth paled by human words, or beauty marred
By mortal vision, must I try to say.
O Great Apollo! Grant the strenuous wing
This ultimate labour needs. This height to sing,
So fit me with thy fashioning hands that I
Win thy loved laurels with a task so hard.
One pinnacle of Parnassus—one till now—
Sufficed me, but the holier heights supply
My needs for this last wrestling-ground. Do thou
Enter and through me breathe such song as that
The wretched Marsyas heard, and quailed till he
Was flayed for his presumption. O Divine!
Wilt thou but implicate thyself in me,
That Heaven's high shadow, on this brain of mine
Imprinted, be in words interpreted!

Then shalt thou crown me at thy chosen tree
With laurels only through this theme and thee
Appropriate to my worth.
                    So seldom shed
Are its fresh leaves to crown triumphant brow
Either of poet or of conqueror
—Such the infirmities of human will
That surely should the Delphic deity
Rejoice when any mortal mind, as now,
Is stirred by the Peneian branch to be
Athirst to wear it.
                    Flames magnificent
May follow from one spark's first feebleness;
And better voices may their prayers address
At Cirrha's sacred mount, to gain for me
Response, who am not worthy.
                    Diversely
Riseth the lantern of the universe
To mortal sight, but most propitiously,
And unioned to a most propitious star,
When the four circles in three crosses meet;
And at that time he will with genial heat
Upon the mundane wax himself impress
Most deeply, tempering to his mood.
                    So here
It was, and at the hour when morning lay
To right, and to the left the evening,
At equal distance, all the hemisphere
Aglow, and all that other dark, when she,
Beatrice, leftward turned, and raised her eyes
Sunward. No eagle could the light absorb
That smote us radiant from the noonday orb
As did she then; and as from light is born
A light reflected, so, in kindred wise,
I caught her gesture, and my weaker eyes
Lifted, beyond our mortal wont, to see

Deep into that pure light's profundity.
Much is there in that higher, holier place
Which is not granted to our mortal race,
Each region having its propriety.
I could not long endure such light, but yet
Such time mine eyes the blinding glory met
That when they fell the sun was around
Shining like molten metal on the ground
Poured from the furnace.
                    Day me seemed to day
Was suddenly added, light to light, as though
God's power had caused a second sun to glow,
Doubling the day's intensity. Mine eyes,
Baffled by this extremity of light,
Turned to Beatrice, whose own gaze remained
Fixed upward on the sky's profundity.
So gazing on her, such new life I gained
As came to Glaucus, when that grass he ate
Which gave the alien freedom of the sea,
And made him comrade of the gods. To me
Came change of life which no humanity
Can either clothe in words, or comprehend.
Let him whom grace will dower so highly wait
Experience for himself.
                    If in that hour
I was no more than that which, new, create,
Invades the body at birth, O Love Divine!
Who in that heaven of light art Absolute Power,
Thou knowest, Who, by that same light didst draw
Myself toward Thee. But whate' er was more
Of soul or physical body, when the wheel
Which thou (by kindling for Thyself desire)
Makest perpetual, caught me up to feel
Its tempered and discriminate harmony,
Such ocean of the intense gold sunlight saw
That rain nor river spread a lake as wide

As now I witnessed of celestial fire.
The sound unheard before, the light unguessed,
Stirred in me for their cause more keen a zest
Than aught I felt in earthlier days; and she
Who saw me rather as herself in me
Than separate, to the unspoken thought replied:
"Thou foilest by thy false imagining
That which were clear to an inferior mind
If it were first from misconception free.
Thou art not on the earth. The lightnings flee
Downward from their high house more laggardly
Than though dost rise a higher place to find."
So briefly to my doubt she smiled reply.
But grounded firmly as my feet she set,
Her answer caught them in a further net.
"From one amazement freed, I marvel now
How my dense weight of flesh can rise so high
Transcending lighter air."
                      I heard her sigh
As might a mother at a child perverse
Beyond restraint of counsel. Patient yet,
She gave me answer: "Of one unity
Is all created in this Universe,
Mutual in all its parts, its form thereby
Alike to God who made it. Creatures blest
By high perception in this norm descry
The Eternal Virtue, source and goal alike
Of all its parts, although not equally
They seek a centre or at height to rest,
But each toward that port which suits it best
Moves through the ocean of reality.
"This urge toward the moon the flame extends,
Is surgent at the heart of things that die,
Doth earthward gravitate all earthly ends,
Nor only rules the unconscious entity,
But those who think and love.

             "This providence,
Assorting all, doth outward still remain,
Serene and spaceless by its light's defence,
The swiftest Heaven containing. That to gain
—The ultimate Heaven of flooded light—we go,
Upshot as by a shaft from God's own bow,
That doth not fail its joyful mark to find.
"Truth is it that the artist's moulding stress
May meet a medium which resists his mind,
Too hard of substance or too lustreless
To be to his creative thought inclined.
And so may creatures of a conscious will
Resist the heavenly call, and swerve aside,
The ardent impulse of ascent to kill
(As fire thrusts downward from the cloud) with vain
Following of false joys,
                "No cause to marvel thine
More at thy rising, than at flame's ascent,
Or at the natural falling of the rain.
It were the wonder should thy course incline
Not upward, from released impediment."
She ceased, who saw me with a mind content;
And turned her eyes to highest heaven again.

CANTO II

Oh ye who in slight skiffs, by music led,
Have to this point among our human dead
Followed my keel upon its singing way,
Take caution now! Your shores are still to see.
Why should you venture on too strange a sea,
Uncharted, untraversed, when, losing me,
You might be left for evermore astray?
Minerva's winds I feel: my course ahead
Apollo guideth: and the Muses nine
Point to the Bears. Ye few who, timely fed
On angels' food (which here must life sustain,
And yet who feedeth leave unsatisfied),
Ye only few may dare this course of mine,
Following the furrow which my tracks divide
Before its hollow sides unite again.
The glorious ones who once to Colchis came,
When Jason turned to ploughman in their sight,
Beheld a thing less marvelled than shall ye.
The natural deathless thirst in heaven to be
—The aspiration all from birth may claim—
Impelled us upward with the speed of light
Wellnigh as fast to rise as eyes could see
Into the luminous vault's immensity,
The while I on Beatrice gazed, and she
Gazed upward.
               In such time as from the bow

A back-drawn shaft upon its course may go,
I came where I beheld a wondrous thing.
And she, who did not miss my wondering,
Turning toward me in such guise that joy
Increased her beauty, and her beauty gave
An added joyance, said: "Thy mind employ
In gratitude to Him by Whom so far
Thou art exalted to the lowliest star."
It seemed a cloud enclosed us, shining, dense,
With polished surface firm that, diamond-bright,
Was dazzling in the sun's reflected light.
We passed within the eternal pearl, as sinks
A ray of sunlight in the stream, which drinks
The light, land is not opened: cleft and whole.
If I were body or unsubstanced soul
I know not. What in wisdom can we guess
Who see one body, not itself the less,
Another in its own dimension take,
Beyond our comprehending? This the more
Should kindle longing to ourselves explore
That essence where, at last the Accepted Bride,
Our nature to High God is unified.
That which we hold by faith we do not state
In logic's terms. We do not demonstrate,
But like the primal truth to man self-known
Accept it, confident in belief. I said:
"Madonna, thanks devout to God I own
Who here hath raised me from the world of sin.
But wilt thou show me what those marks may be
Which on this moon's bright surface duskily
When men look upward from the earth they see,
And tell the tale of Cain?"
                        Then mirthfully,
She smiled upon me. "Now," she said, "no more
The shafts of wonder should thy mind transfix
That mortal wisdom fails without the key

Of sense by which to enter. Here you see
That even where the senses lead, the wings
Of reason are too short. But tell me first
Thine own interpretation."
                                   I to her:
"I judge that bodies more or less dispersed
In this high region, by their density,
Or else deffuseness, differing aspects bear
To those on earth who view them."
                                          "Verily,"
She answered, "wilt thou hearken now to me,
Thy thought, confronted by mine argument,
Shall own its falsehood.
"The eighth sphere displays
A multitude of glories, variously
Perceived, not only through their quantities,
But by their qualities also. If their rays
Were different only as their density
Should vary, then one virtue, more or less,
Were in them only. Diverse virtues spring
From diverse principles. Of all of these
There were one only by thy reasoning.
"And think again, if differing densities
Cause the bright surface or the duskier blur,
Either the tenuous patch continues through
The moon's whole substance, or alternately,
Like fat and lean the different strata lie.
"Were the first true, the sun's eclipse would show
With penetrating light, which is not so,
And therefore, if the next I overthrow,
Thy theory wholly is reject. If through
The moon's opaqueness naught of sunlight drives
From the far side, then reason bids infer
That somewhere, through its whole circumference,
There is a limit to the rarity
For which you argue; and, if this be so,

From such dark stratum must the light recoil,
As colour backward from a glass is thrown
By lead behind it. Yet you will not lack
The final argument that further back
May be the density by which the patch
Shows darker; but from this abortive plea
Experiment will disentangle thee,
If that thou pleasest, as thine arts are known
To advocate, for from experiments spring
The streams of knowledge ever broadening.
"Three mirrors shalt thou take, exposing two
At equal distance, and the third, between,
Ranged further from thine eyes. Behind thy back
Kindle a torch from which they shall return
Reflected light toward thee. Smaller seen
Will be the further, but as bright to view
As those more near on either hand.
                              "And now
-Thine own false reasons both dissolved, as snow
Melts in the sunlight to the equal lack
Of colour and coldness—I would more inform
Thy bankrupt intellect with light so warm,
So living, it shall vibrate in thy sight.
"Within the heavens of holy peace revolves
A body from whose virtue is derived
The being of all which they contain. The height
Of the near heaven above, which hath to show
So many constellations, diverse-bright,
Hath diverse essences distributed
Among them, which themselves by various glow
Distinguish in their own diversity.
So also through the graded heavens rotate
A Myriad circling bodies of diverse state,
By various powers divine impregnated,
With downward influence from above them fed.
"Now mark intently how the truth I thread

To that thou seekest, that the ford alone
Thy feet may take hereafter. Impulsed thus
They wheel, and on mankind they operate—
As doth the hammer that the smith controls,
His art, and not its own, to justify.
The shining constellations, marvellous
From the deep Mind from which their circle rolls,
Marked by its seal upon them, must impress
The image that themselves accept no less
Upon the earth beneath. And as men's souls
Emerge from out their animated dust
Through different members diversely designed
For various operations, so the Mind
Divine, the myriad diverse stars behind,
Deploys its virtue, each diversion free
Within its comprehensive unity.
"As in yourself glad life the dust inspires
To various functions, so the Soul Divine
Inspires the constellations, shining, through
As from your eyes the spring of life in you
Shines outward. Hence, and not from dense or rare,
Complexions of the different stars compare
So variously; their lights derived from whence
Is every manner of all excellence.

CANTO III

The Sun which warmed me first to fair Love's heat
Had now revealed me Truth, as bare, as sweet,
By proof and by disproof interpreted;
And I thereat, to own in measure meet
That I was throughly answered, raised my head,
Intending speech. But such a sight was mine
To hold me straightly to itself, that I
Forgot my purpose. As translucent glass,
Or shallow water where the light will pass
Clear to the bottom, mirrors those who gaze.
Faint as a white pearl on as white a brow,
So there were many faces round me now
Eager for speech. Narcissus' error here
My sight reversed. I thought: 'Reflections shine
Of those who stand behind me'. Round I turned;
But naught beheld, and from that mystery
Altered my glance mine own sweet guide to see;
And glowing in those sacred eyes I met
A smile at my confusion.
                        "Wonder not,"
She said: "that in mine eyes is merriment,
Seeing thee thus thy timid feet withdraw
From the firm ground, preferring vacancy,
Thy childlike wont in all things. Those you see
Are truest substance; relegated here
For failure of their vows of chastity.

Speak with them: heed: believe. The verity
Of light with which their souls are satisfied
Allows not that they turn their feet aside
From truth's conclusions."
                    I thereat, to one
Who seemed most eager to converse, began:
"O well-created Spirit, who dost feel
That sweetness which can never words reveal
To those who have not tasted life divine,
Intense, eternal—joy to hear were mine
If thou wouldst tell thy name, and show the lot
You share with your companions."
                            She thereon
Gave me a glance that with glad radiance shone,
And smiled assent: "Our love refuseth not
So fair a wish. As prompt it drops the bar
As to the courts of God the gateways are
Made wide to those who would Love's likeness share.
I was a Sister, sworn to chastity,
Not stranger to thee once. Of right I wear
A greater beauty now, but search with care
Thy memory, and this radiance shall not be
Impenetrable. Piccarda once was I,
Who, with the blessed ones around me here,
Am stationed in this slowest-moving sphere.
"Our passions now no lowlier flame can know
Than of the Holy Spirit by which we glow,
Informed by that celestial mystery,
And in that form exulting.
                        "This low spot
Is given to us whose vows continued not
Inviolate from the world's assault."
                                I said:
"From God such glowing splendour now transmutes
Your previous beauty that my mind delayed
In recollection of its old conceits.

But now, through its most radiant attributes,
Thy face is evident that before I knew.
But tell me, ye who bide so lowly here,
Have ye no longing for the loftier seats,
The more of Heaven to see, or dwell more dear,
And closer to the Highest?"
                        A smile at this
Lightened her eyes, and those who crowded near
Smiled with her. Then she spoke, and all the bliss
Of Love's first flame, it seemed, was hers to sing,
She was so joyous in her answering.
"Brother, the quality of our Love doth still
The impulse of rebellion; all our will
Being God's only. Here we rest content.
What God hath in his perfect counsel meant
In our assorting is our certain good.
Incapable of a different thirst are we,
And, that you may the clear occasion see,
Consider that Love rules omnipotent
From threshold unto threshold, from this low
Soon-circling moon, that for our home we know,
To the vast Ultimate Heaven. And think again.
What is Love's nature? Love itself were vain
If envy could corrupt it. Love must be
Surrender by its own necessity
Unto the God from Whom itself derives.
No more desire in emulation strives,
But all our joy is in this will supreme;
And thence is His joy also, that our wills
Find peace in His—the universal sea
Which to Itself all that Itself creates,
And all that Nature thence originates,
Draws in divine attraction."
                            So to me
Came understanding of how Heaven fulfils
Its Paradise entire, although the grace

Of the Chief Good is not in every place
Rained down in like abundance. But, as when
One food is eaten to satiety
While appetite remains, the while we say
Thanks for the platter that is moved away,
In the same breath we ask a different dish,
So I with pleading gesture spoke my wish
That she should draw the shuttle further through,
To the web's end. And she replied thereto:
"Now heavened in a loftier place than I
Is one who once beneath your earthly sky
Came to high merit and life perfected;
Who founded that veiled rule of those whose vows
That they till death will take the Heavenly Spouse
To lie beside them only, He doth bless
With glorious acceptance, if no less
Of love than Heaven requires impel their vow.
"While girlhood yet was green the world I fled,
Following the passion that she taught. To Wed
The cloister only was I vowed. I wore
The habit of her order. But to me
Came men more prone to ill than good. They tore
My hands reluctant from that hold: the shame
God knoweth that my later life became.
"And she beside me, whose bright spirit doth shine,
On my right hand, with all the light divine
Our sphere contains, accepts this tale of mine
For herself also. She alike was vowed:
She also ravished from that sisterhood
By the sharp violence of her closest kind;
Yet when the shadow of the sacred veil
Drew from her, and reluctant use allowed
Inferior pleasure, still her heart withstood
The sieges of the world. It dwelt behind
The veil of its own chastity. Her light
Is that of Constance, once of worldly height,

Who, to the second blast of Suabia,
Bore him who was the third and final might."
So said she, and her speech was turned to song,
Ave Maria, and the while she sang
She faded from my sight, as sinks a stone
In the dark water's depth. Mine eyes so long
As sight allowed pursued her. Left alone
I sought anew my keen need, and turned
Toward Beatrice, but so brightly burned
Her glance upon me that my sight declined
Endurance of its light at first to find,
Which made me tardier in my questioning.

CANTO IV

Being set between two foods, exactly alike
To call of appetite, exactly placed
At equal distance from his reach, a man
Might starve before his hungry teeth should taste
Of either banquet, while desire would pull
Two ways at once with similar strength; and so
A lamb between two ravening wolves might show
No motion either right or left to go,
In equapoise of terror; or a hound
Between two hinds in cloven doubt might stand,
And both find safety from its lust to kill.
And therefore if no present words I found
Vext by perplexities on either hand
Of equal urgence, my defect of will
I blame not, nor defend. My peace I held;
But on my face desire was painted so
That words would never with so warm a glow
Have made petition; and Beatrice took
The part of Daniel when he read the dream
Before he gave its meaning, which dispelled
The misdirected wrath that made the King
Unjustly cruel.
            "Yes," she said, "I see
How two desires at once entangle thee
That neither comes to previous birth. 'If will,'
Your mind protests, 'be constant to the good,

Although frustrated from the thing it would,
How can ulterior violence rightfully
Reduce its measure of desert?'

       "And still
More gallful is thy next perplexity,
Which sees the souls, as Plato's doctrine said,
Heavened in their stars, and so, to ease thy doubt,
I treat it first. Of all the seraphim,
Not he to God the closest—Samuel,
Moses or John—not Mary herself, doth dwell
In higher heaven than those thine eyes have seen,
Nor different timing of their years hath been,
Nor will be. None God's circle stays without,
Nor fails its beauties to augment. They share
The same sweet life with difference, each aware
Of its own narrow portion of the same
Eternal Inspiration. That they here
Are visible to thee, does not mean this sphere
Contains them, but informs thee that they claim
The least celestial eminence. Needs must be
That speech they use, to reach your faculty
Of apprehension, that your senses bring
In fashioned tribute to the intellect,
As doth the Scripture, showing God erect,
Manlike, with feet and hands; so furnishing
An image that profounder meaning veils.
And so the Church's teaching represents
Gabriel and Michael in the guise of men,
And Tobit's healer.

      "Timaeus' argument
—Be literal value to his words applied—
Swerves from the truth I tell thee, for he saith
That spirits to their own stars return at death,
As to a dwelling which they only left
When Nature from the eternal matrix cleft
That which should animate an earthly clay.

Yet haply words from meaning branched away,
Intending truth no wisdom should deride;
That influence, from their starry hosts which came
For honour or dishonour, praise or blame,
Returns unto them when its work is done.
"So may his shaft a truth have reached; but yet
This truth misunderstood the world hath set,
Almost the whole voice of the world, astray,
To call on Jupiter and Mars, as they
Were ultimate gods..
    "Thy next perplexity
Hath less of venom, for it could not lead
Thy mind to leave me, though our justice seem
Unjust by mortal standards, as you say.
It is not hectic iniquity
That marvels of the heavenly truth you see
Which foils your understanding. Faith's debate
Is here; and since your mind hath wit to read,
I will expound it to you. Violence
Implies that he who suffers naught submits,
And naught contributes, to his loss. But those
With whom you spoke were partial to oppose
Their wills to that which wrought their vows' offence.
For, if the will be constant, soon or late
Resistance triumphs. Can a flame be bent
So that it will not straighten? Wrench it down
A thousand times, it will not rest content
Until it rise again its natural way.
But if it bend itself, it doth abet
The violence which assaults it, though it be
Reluctant of the deed; and thus did they.
"For had their will retained that constancy
Which held St Lawrence to the grid, and made
Mucius against his own hand obdurate,
They had reverted to the holy state
So soon as rapine loosed them. But too rare

Is such inflexibility of will
To rout the violence of the world
                              "Yet still,
Though I have rendered void thine argument,
I see before thine eyes a straighter doubt,
Where thou shouldst weary ere the way were won,
If thou shouldst take it lonely. Sure is set
This truth upon thy mind, that never one
Of all the blessed can be cast without
The Ultimate Height of Heaven, who faithfully
Held to the primal truth; but thou hast heard
From Piccarda a different-seeming word,
That Constance in devotion did not swerve
From that which godless violence tore away.
"But many a time, my brother, men may see
Thing done unseemly, other ills to flee,
As did Alcmaeon, at his father's prayer,
His mother's life destroy. Behold a son
Impious from filial piety! And so
May violence work upon the will that none
May call it guiltless. Of its fear aware,
It doth not willingly consent to go,
Yet is in choice consenting, to avoid
Some wrong by which it might be worse annoyed.
Piccarda spoke of the uninfluenced will,
And I of that which bent to circumstance:
With difference thus a single truth we show."
So copiously the stream of truth outwelled
Upon me, from the Eternal Spring that held
All truth for its subservance. Sated now
Were both my longings.
                    "O Divine!" I said,
"Love of the Primal Lover! By thy speech
My thirst is overflowed, my hunger fed,
My spirit livened. But I may not reach
To give thee grace for grace; I can but pray

That what my poor love hath no depths to pay
He Who hath all will grant thee. This I see:
Truth will be sought without satiety
Unless that Truth which doth all truth contain
Illume and guide it to its end; and then
It rests, as some wild creature finds its den,
And sinks to satisfaction. This I see:
That though the mind may wander homelessly,
It need not find at last futility,
But the den waits its patience.
     "Wherefore spring
Around truth's feet these shoots of questioning,
Of the blind mould impatient. Ridge by ridge
They urge us to the summit. This doth give
Reverent assurance to my mind to place
Another doubt, that I am weak to bridge,
Before thee for solution. Of thy grace,
Inform me if a man can satisfy
Demands of heaven with other merchandise,
So that the short weight of a broken vow
May not his hope confound."
     Beatrice now
Looked at me with such love in such bright eyes
That I might not sustain in any wise
Their beams to meet: mine insufficiency
From that loved heaven so low rejected me.

CANTO V

Then, to interpret that divine regard,
She first made answer: "If it seem too hard
The flame of love-born beauty to sustain,
So that your dazzled eyes contend in vain
Against a greater warmth than earth can know,
Of this thing make no marvel. It is born
From vision of the food, which apprehends
More than is possible to earthly eyes;
And, with its sight, its own advance extends
Toward the apprehended. As you rise,
Somewhat I see your earthly mind replies,
Heating itself at the eternal light,
Which, as it breaks upon your mortal sight,
Must love enkindle to the like degree.
"If aught beside on earth your love seduce
It is from this same source that breaketh through,
Misapprehended though that source may be.
"But for the question that you ask me now,
Can man, you doubt, redeem a broken vow
With other service, that his final state
Be at God's judgement sure beyond debate?"
So Beatrice put my doubt, and straight
Went on to its solution.
                        "Many gifts
God gave at the creation, from a hand
Most full, and freely opened. Best of all,

Most near to His own nature, and which lifts
Man nearest to Himself, the boon he planned
Was freedom of the will, with which he dowered
The intelligent creation, severally,
As in united action.
                    "Hence will be
A vow's high value evident to thee
-If from my premise you deduce aright—
Providing only that when man consents
God consent also. For the tribute made
By such surrender is in coinage paid
Most precious, as I showed, and in the act
Itself is evidenced. What thus can be
In substitution for such covenants
Adequate to offer? If you think to use
To different purpose that you pledged, you plan
Of stolen goods to make your husbandry.
"So are you answered on the major count.
But since the church will dispensation give,
Which seems assertion of the contrary,
You needs must longer at the table sit,
As one who, eating a rebellious food,
Requires more patience for digesting it.
"Bend thou thy thoughts to fix the thing I show;
For to perceive a thing and not retain
Is to divert the mind, but naught to know.
"Two matters to the sacrifice pertain:
That which is vowed, and the contracting vow.
The second can no loosened bond allow:
It was of that I spoke in words precise.
Observe, that Hebrews should make sacrifice
Was law beyond exception, but the gift
They laid upon the altar was not so
Fixed beyond changing. Likewise may the vow
Be varied in its sacrifice. But yet
No private judgement should be bold to shift

The burden that the shoulders bear. For he
Will need the white key and the yellow key
That door to open to his soul's release.
And such surrender, for his after-peace
He yet may count as folly, if no more
He yield than he recover. Six to four
Should be the basis of that bargaining.
"It follows that if man shall consecrate
So much to God that it the scale shall tip
Against whatever else of worth he bring,
There can be no redemption. Can he try
A trade for that he hath no means to buy?
"Let no man make to God a random vow,
Look first with steady eyes, and truth allow.
Remember Jephthah, who had done less ill
To own his vow unrighteous than to kill
His daughter, as though God could give consent
To any vow that slew the innocent.
"Such was the fault that Iphigenia wept
When the Greek Leader foully vowed, and kept
The vow best broken. That her face was fair
Brought her to death that sage and simple there
Lamented vainly.
                "Men of Christ should be
Apt to no vow except with gravity,
Not feathers every wind can sweep aside,
Not thinking they are cleansed by every tide.
You have the Old and the New testament
For guidance, and the Church's pastoral care.
Let them be your salvation. But beware
Of evil shepherds, led by avarice,
Who offer pardons at an easier price.
Be men, not sheep; lest that ye think and do
Become the mockery of the Christless Jew."
At that Beatrice ceased, and every word
Was printed on my mind, that all I heard

I here can write. She raised her eyes toward
That point from which the earth most quickeneth,
With evident aspiration. As the cord
Still trembles while the loosened shaft hath struck,
So instant to the second realm we rose.
And as we entered that superior sphere
So gladdened did my lady's face appear
That the whole star responsive glowed. Conceive
If the star waked to laughter, what did I,
Used at each trivial change to laugh or grieve
At dictates of my frail mortality.
As when a fishpond's surface tranquil-clear
Is broken by some substance thrown, and they
Who think of food from every side appear
Drawing toward it, so did every way
A thousand splendours close around us now.
And from each spirit came a voice that cried:
"Lo, one by whom our loves are magnified!"
And each, approaching, by an effluent glow
Cast out toward us, did the gladness show
That filled it.
              Reader, if my tale should stay,
And naught be told thee of my upward way
Through Heaven, till then unseen by mortal eyes,
Think how thy thwarted questionings would rise
In protest at the dearth my silence gave;
And think therefrom with what keen thirst I longed
To hear from these of what their state might be.
"Oh, blest at birth!"—From these who round me thronged
A voice addressed me—"Thou by grace allowed
The Thrones of the Triumphant here to view
Ere thine own time of earthly strife be through,
We by the light that ranges Heaven are lit,
And therefore, if you seek some share of it,
Fear no refusal here, but ask aloud."
Thereat Beatrice spoke: "Abandon fear.

Ask freely what you will; and what you hear
Believe as from the lips of gods it came."
"Truly," I answered to the spirit who spake,
"I see thou hast that light of heavenly flame.
It sparkles through thine eyes that fall on me.
But who thou art I may not guess, nor see
Why thou art graded here in Mercury,
Which in the sun's light hides itself from men."
So spoke I; and that spirit exceeded then
Its previous brightness. As the sun will rise
Mist-reddened, but will chase the vapours down
By its victorious heat, and clearer skies
Will mount, invested with too bright a crown
For mortal eyes to meet it, so excelled
That spirit in light through crescent ecstasies,
Garmented and regarmented with light:
And answered in the words which next I write.

CANTO VI

"When Constantine had led the eagle back
Nearly the whole course of the westward track
Of him of old who took Lavinia,
A hundred and a hundred years and more
The bird of God abode on Europe's shore,
Facing the mountains whence at first he flew.
And there beneath his sacred wings anew
The world he ruled and sheltered. Constantine
Died, and from hand to hand the imperial power
Passed with the change of years, and came to mine.
Caesar I was, and am Justinian,
Who, being prompted by the Primal Cause
Which all pervades me in this holier hour,
Pruned off abortive and redundant laws.
"One time, before my zeal that work began,
I held the heretic belief that one,
One nature only, was in God the Son,
And was content with his divinity.
But Agapetus (God's high pastor he)
By clearer teaching caused mine eyes to see
The truth entire, as plain as is to you
That contradictions are both false and true.
And soon, as with the Church I moved my feet,
God of his grace inspired me to complete
That task, on which the more to concentrate
To Belisarius the imperial fate,

So far as safety must on arms depend,
I wholly trusted. Heaven's right hand in that
Was stretched to aid me with such evident will
As signalled approbation. So I fill
Requirement of thy first request; but more
Its matter makes demand. That thou mayst see
With how much of good right proceedeth he
Who to his own hand doth appropriate
The Holy Standard, and how much is his
Who doth oppose him, thou shalt contemplate
Its sum of virtue which for reverence
Hath made it worthy, from that earliest day
When Pallas died to plant it.
     "Thou dost know
How first in Alba for three centuries
It ruled, until the strife of three with three
Its fate decided. Then through seven reigns,
From the raped Sabines to Lucretia's woe,
Thou knowest further the high deeds it wrought,
Brennus and Pyrrhus, and what tale besides
Of mighty princes and confederacies,
From which Torquatus' lofty fame derived,
And that of Quinctius of the combless hair,
The Decii and the Fabii, each of whom
I joy to place within the embalming tomb
Of song which will not fail.
     "It overthrew
The swarming Afric host that Hannibal's pride
Led through the glacial Alpine rocks from where
The Po comes swiftly down. Beneath its wing
Scipio and Pompeii in their youth excelled,
With bitter consequence to that stern hill
That overlooks thy birthplace.
     "Nigh the time
When the all-brooding heavens designed to bring
The whole world to their own serenity,

It came to the first Caesar's hand, and he,
By Rome's volition, wrought from Var to Rhone,
What knoweth Isere and Arar, and all the Seine,
And every valley of those hills that yield
Their tributes to the Rhone. But after that,
When from Ravenna he crossed the Rubicon,
So soared its sunward flight, to equal it
Not any tongue can speak, nor word be writ.
"Upon Iberia next its host it wheeled,
And then against Durazzo, and thereon
So smote Pharsalia that the Nile's hot shore
Was not too distant to lament the blow.
The eyrie of its birth it saw once more,
Antandros and Simois, and, below,
The grave where Hector lies. An angry wind
Raising again, with death to Ptolemy,
It smote, as lightning smites, Numidia's king.
"Then westward with swift flight it rushed again
Where the Pompeian trumpets shrilled in Spain.
Raised in a different hand, its destiny
Prevailed. Perugia and Modena knew;
And Brutus with his Cassius howls in hell.
When from the asp she took the swift black night
Rather than feel its capturing Claws. It bore
Its peace at last unto the Red Sea shore—
A peace become so absolute, so wide,
That Janus' temple closed.
 "But all before
Wrought by the standard that I boast is naught—
Its brightness dusk, its splendours mean to see—
Regarded with pure heart and clarity,
Beside the terrible vengeance which it did
In the third Caesar's hand. For surely He,
That Living Justice which is life in me,
Inspired him to it as his instrument.
Regard the two-fold marvel! Christ was sent

To feel the vengeance of God, sin's punishment,
And then to Titus was the glory given
To avenge the vengeance for the ancient sin.
"So passed the years. And when the Lombard bit
Into the Church's side, to rescue it
Came the victorious might of Charlemagne,
Beneath the holy ensign's wings to win.
"Now for thyself a judgement make of those
Whom lately I accused of separate sin.
Behold these evils, source of all your woes!
One to the national standard doth oppose
The golden lilies of France, and one doth strain
Its use to be a faction's flag. 'Tis hard
To say who most offendeth. Ghibellines,
Work your designs beneath some different flag!
For lightly may the crowd's allegiance lag
To follow one you have no claim to show.
Nor may the present Charles his Guelphs sustain,
Impious, to drag so great a symbol low.
Let him yet fear the ancient claws that tore
The pelt from many a mightier lion than he.
"Often have children wailed a father's crime,
But let him not suppose at any time
That God the imperial bird will trade away
For those bright lilies which his arms display.
"This small low star on which we meet contains
Good spirits passionate in pursuit of fame
And honour of earthly life, and hence desires
May swerve so far that strength which love requires
Is somewhat lessened for its mounting rays.
But yet no less we give to God the praise,
No less perceive that our deserts and gains
Are justly measured in the perfect scale.
For in us the live justice doth prevail,
And malice may not warp affections here.
"As varying voices make sweet harmony

On earth, so is it this holier sphere.
Degrees of difference make one song entire;
And various flames construct one wheel of love.
"Within this present pearl that Romeo
Shineth whose heel Provencal envy bit
For his most noble work designed and done.
But he, by then who had completed it,
So dealt that the last laughter doth not go
To those whose malice sought his overthrow.
"Four daughters had Duke Raymond, and no son,
Yet each of these became a high princess,
One England's queen, one France's queen; no less
The others to great honour. This was done
By Romeo's wisdom, to Provence who came
A stranger, with a pilgrim's lowliness,
And with a pilgrim's poverty. When disfame
Whispered against him, charging fraud and greed,
So that his lord required a count be made
If any treasure in his hand had stayed,
He more than justly rendered, twelve for ten,
And that no slander in the mouths of men
Might live thereafter, took his mule and staff,
And left that court as naked as he came,
All gifts contemning. Nay, not theirs the laugh.
"But had the world known in what heart he went
In poverty and age from door to door,
Begging by crust and crust his meagre store,
Much as it praiseth, it had praised him more.

CANTO VII

"Lord God of Sabaoth, Holiest and Most High,
Hosanna to the sacred Name we praise
Which by its superlustrous light's descent
Doth kindle all this heavenly firmament
With penetrant fire divine."
                    I heard him raise
This chant triumphant—he, that Being blest
On whom twin lights in doubled glory rest,
The purifier both of rule and law.
A moment only he and those I saw
Who like himself danced to the sacred strain,
And then, as sudden sparks to darkness fly,
The distance hid them.
                    "Ask her—ask," I said
Within myself, "entreat her to supply
That living water of truth which twice before
My thirst hath sated." But I bent my head
As one oblivious. Diffident fear was more
Restraint than love of truth was urgence now.
But well she knew how reverence overcame
My difficult speech, and how my head must bow
To but one syllable of her worshipped name,
And short the time she left me thus. A smile
Shone from her eyes upon me, such as well
Might make men blissful in the flames of hell;
And then she spoke: "My thought, which doth not err,

Perceives thy question. *Be the vengeance just,
Can vengeance for that vengeance justly be?*
That query might be answered speedily;
But give me all thy mind, and thou shalt hear
Full revelation of this mystery.
"Because one man, who was not born, declined
Contentment in a wise restraint to find,
Himself he damned, and all his flesh that grew
From him by natural process: all alike
One flesh, one sin. So lay the human crew
In deathly sickness many a century,
Deluded by its own conceits, till He
The Immortal Word of God, that nature drew,
That fallen nature, to Himself anew,
By the sole act of his eternal love.
"Consider this: That nature, reallied
To Him Who made it, cleansed and deified,
Was perfect, sinless as Himself; but yet
Was that same nature which the gates had set
Of Paradise barred against it: its own act
Repudiating its appointed way
Of truth, its life intended. If we weigh
The nature which endured the cross, we say
That never was a juster penalty.
But if the Person who that nature bore
Our judgement ponder, then the punishment
Appears most monstrous. Mark the twofold fact.
God at that deed rejoiced: rejoiced the Jews.
Earth quaked. The outraged heavens open tore.
Perceive the dual truths, and doubt no more
The justice that condemned what God designed.
"But now I see, from thought to thought, thy mind
Maked further question. 'What I hear,' you say,
'Is clear to comprehension. But I see
Not plainly why that only mode should be
The path of our redemption! This decree,

Brother, is mystery to all eyes but those
Which at Love's feet have learnt their litany.
"But since this target draws most shafts which fall
At middle distance, hear the truth that shows
This method worthiest of a choice divine:
Glowing within itself, God's excellence,
Contemning envy where no equal is,
Radiates abroad its everlasting light,
And the assertion of its loveliness
Hath not the finite bound of more or less;
Nor can it be reversed; nor where its seal
Hath stamped God's image, any subsequent night
Obliterate that eternal signature.
"That which down-floweth from this source is free,
Unmeasured, not to mutability
Made subject. As its inspiration pure
Shows us most likeness, so in men must be
Most conquering life; and as they fail therefrom,
Though by but one ray of the eternal light,
They are reduced in their nobility.
"Sin only hath this power, from men to take
The secret likeness of the Eternal Good,
So that their nature with a glow less bright
Return the eternal brilliance. Never more
May it re-enter through that closing door,
Excepting, for the void it digged, it make
Full bulk of reparation: false delight
Being full balanced by just penalty.
"And so, when sinned the first including seed,
Which was mankind in its totality,
Not only Paradise was lost: the night
Sank also on the heavenly dignity
Which was man's previous nature. How shall be
This loss recovered? Ask thyself, and heed
The inevitable answer.
    "What shall pass

This gulf of separation? Only here
Two possible fords across its depth appear,
That either God in sole benignity
Shall without satisfaction all remit,
Or man shall compensation make.
                              "Now fix
Intent thine eyes upon the deep abyss
Of the eternal counsel! Man for this
Was powerless. Could he find humility
Sufficient to abase himself as low
As his false pride had risen, when he defied
The rule of his Creator? Surely no.
And therefore was he hopeless to redeem
Himself from condemnation. Needs must be
That God alone of his own potency
Should the maimed life to heavenly rights restore,
Or both fords in divine duality
Employ for its salvation. God must choose,
The way most Godlike. Every deed the more
Is gracious as itself is pregnated.
With the heart's bounty which itself conceived.
And therefore the Divine Beneficence
Chose the most Godlike mode, Itself to lose
That men might profit: stamping its design
Even on the fallen image that gave offence.
"Not since the first day dawned, until shall fall
The shades of the last night across the sky,
Nay, nor thenceafter, any deed of all
Shall match with this in height of majesty.
God needs must choose the method most divine,
Equal to this. For our redemption He
Bent to the burden of humanity.
"Now, to relieve thy final doubt, which says:
'I see the water, and I see the fire,
The fluid air, the solid earth I see,
And all their mixtures. But what substance stays?

What is their end but mutability?'
I answer this: Although your mind perceived
Apparent contradiction, when I called
All things created incorruptible,
And the material earth abundant shows
The workings of corruption, not indeed
Is contradiction here. This heavenly land,
Brother, with all its sinless angel band,
These may be called created, through and through.
But those base elements observed by you
Are rather by created virtue formed,
Its temporary expression, not itself;
And so the life of plant and brute is warmed
From the out-sparkling of the sacred stars
Thrown downward or withdrawn. But life of thine
Is breathed immediate from the Source Divine,
So that, divorced therefrom, you upward yearn,
And furthest wandering would most fain return.
And hence, if thou recall how first the flesh
That is mankind was kneaded, thou canst see
Good reason for the further life to be."

CANTO VIII

The world of men in times now ancient
Held that the Cyprian from her native star
Rained down on earth her love incontinent.
Wherefor they praised her and her amorous care
With blood of sacrifice and votive cry;
And not her only in their false belief
They worshipped, but alike to Dione,
Being her mother, and to Cupid, he
Being her son, their hymns they raised. They told
How once he sat on Dido's knees. They saw
Her dwelling in the star that, overbold,
Twice daily, night and morning, courts the sun.
I knew not, till the upward course was done,
That I that star had gained, but then the law
That makes thereon all beauty manifold
Revealed it to me in Beatrice's eyes,
Which not till then had been in anywise
So lovely, though their previous loveliness
Surpassed inadequate words of earth.
                                     Hast seen
A spark transgress a steadier flame? Hast heard
A voice of constant volume, word by word,
Disturbed by one which alters? So I saw
Lights in that light which torchlike danced, their pace
Varying, I think, through all eternity
According as its vision was theirs. From Him

That cincture which is first the Seraphim
So spirals downward to this circling race.
But now so rapidly from their line they broke
That from cold cloud the invisible thunder-stroke
Falls not so fast. So swift to us they came
That by their motion would the lightning lag;
And from the vanward of their front of flame
Hosanna pealed in such sweet melody
That never shall I shake the longing free
Again to hear it.
                    One advanced more near
Than came those others. "All who meet thee here,"
He said, "are servants to thy will, to make
Thy joy's occasion. Principalities
Are here who in one circle roll: who slake
One thirst, which thou thyself didst indicate,
Writing on earth: *Oh, ye, whose ecstasies
Give the Third Heaven its moving life*. In us
Love moves so regnant that to pleasure thee
Is sweet as our suspended dance could be."
I raised at first mine eyes in reverence
Toward my Lady to enquire her will,
And having her assurance, turned them thence
To that glad spirit proffering to fulfil
My asking with the prodigality
To which love urged it. "Tell me who you be,"
I said, with ardour like his own, and he
Glowed with exceeding pleasure thereat, intense
Of light beyond conception. Changing thus,
He answered: "Short the space the world below
Confined me fleshly. Had it not been so,
Much evil had been spared which yet must be.
Joy is it that conceals my form from thee,
A rose out-radiant: like a creature clad
In silk, its own creation. Love you had
Onetime for me, with likely cause, for lo!

Had life endured, I had not failed to show
More than the flowerless leaves of love for thee.
"The left bank of the Rhone, anear the sea,
After it takes the Sorga, looked to me
To be its lord at the appropriate hour,
As did that corner of Ausonia
Which hath three cities for its diadem
Bari, Gaeta, and Catona, where
Tronto and Verde mingle with the sea.
Already on my brows two crowns of power
Shone bright. Those banks the Danube's waters sweep,
After they leave the German lands, were mine,
And soon alike would fair Trinacria,
Which between Pachynus and Pelorus
Darkens above the gulf tormented most
By Eurus (not for wrath of Typhoeus,
But for the sulphur that ariseth there)
Have looked to have its future kings through me
From Charles and Rudolf spring, had not the scourge
Of evil lordship, which doth break the tie
Of prince and subject, roused Palermo's cry
From streets heart-broken: *Die, thou tyrant, die.*
And, had my brother in good time allowed
His heart to ponder that which all may see
Of Catalonia's greedful poverty,
The sails of flight upon his barque to crowd
He had not loitered: even furtherfold
Will evil cargo weight its cumbered hold,
Unless his own or other's wits provide
Some swift remede. His close parsimony
—Mean sapling seeded from a generous tree!—
Will soon have need of different soldiery
From those who make their aim his chests to fill."
I answered: "Surely am I satisfied
That what I see, you too, with Heaven to guide,
See likewise: rather say, twice joyed am I

Not only that thyself, but Heaven most high
Accords in this conclusion. Joy supplied;
Give wisdom also if thou wilt. Reveal,
I pray thee, how sweet seed of earthly stem
Can bring forth bitter."
                Thus he answered me:
"If I expose a single thought to thee
Thy doubt is ended: that which lies behind
Will meet thy vision. The revolving Good,
That through this whole realm which thou now dost climb
Permeates, with virtue fills these spheres. In them
It makes provision, being itself sublime,
Perfect for all the creatures you will find
Various in each; not only to exist,
But blissful to abide, that all subsist
Not as by random chance, but orderly,
As shafts that reach the mark which He designed
Who loosed them from the bowstring. Else would be
Chaos in Heaven itself, and art divine
Blurred and confused thereby, defaced and wrecked.
And could that be, except the intellect
That moves these stars should have a like defect?
And could that be except the Primal One,
Whose hand should fail his creatures to direct,
Should be Himself defective? Have I done?
Or must I sate you with more argument?"
And I thereat: "You have no need to say
A further word thereon, for well I see
Nothing in Nature can imperfect be
To execute its mission."
                He went on:
"Then tell me: Would men walk the harder way
Were they uncitied and uncivilised?"
I answered: "Surely that is evident.
For that I ask no reason."
                "Then reflect.

How could that be, except that men direct
Efforts diverse to different ends, and so
Be various in their lives and offices?
Your Master wrote of this, and answered: No."
So far he led me on by argument,
Logically deducing point from point, but now
He reached conclusion: "Therefore one is born
A lawyer, Solon; one is Xerxes; one
A priest, Melchizedek; and one is he
Who, soaring vainly sunward, lost his son.
"For that which seeks a mortal tenement
From the revolving Source of life, is not
To one selected fleshly home assigned,
But, by the wisdom of the Eternal Mind,
Indifferent where it find the hostelry
Which it can enter, and its seal impress
On the soft wax of human infancy.
"Esaua from Jacob's seed was sundered thus,
And from such Sire was gendered Quirinus
That Mars was called his father. Time would see
Son following sire in long monotony
Were they not varied by divine decree,
As thus I have expounded.
                     "Now thy doubt
Is silenced. That which lay behind is brought
Beneath thy vision. If I answer more
It shows how greatly I delight in thee.
—With this corollary I gird thee round:
If Nature find in aught disharmony,
As seed that falleth on unfertile ground
She makes that birth abortive. Every flower
Blooms, if at all, in its propitious hour.
And if your world had equal wit to see
The meaning of this lesson, it would be
With those who serve its needs more satisfied.
But he whose hand the sword-hilt fits they rear

To pray within the cloister, while the spear
They force into a nerveless hand. A king
They make of him whose gift is oratory,
And of the studious make a strengthless king.
So is the firm road vacant, while they tire
Alongside, foiled in uncongenial mire.

CANTO IX

Thy Charles, fair Clemence, thus enlightened me;
And more he told, of how deception's snares
Should trammel his descendants; but he said
Thereafter: "Tell ye naught, for who would spread
A net revealed beforehand?" Silenced thus
I say no more than that just Heaven prepares
A well-bought wailing to avenge thy woe.
But now the sphere of love had turned to meet
The effluent source of all its genial heat,
The sun's high glory, ample to bestow
All that is good through Heaven that all things know.
(Ah, souls deluded, creatures impious!
Who from such light can twist your souls aside
To the vain joys that sin's low tempests hide.)
And in that dawn another splendour shone
Toward me, by its more intensity
Of outward brilliance speaking its desire
For converse. Licensed by Beatrice's eyes,
I answered: "O Blest Spirit! Reveal to me,
I charge thee, whom thou art, that I to thee
May make my thought transparent."
                                     Then that fire,
Which yet I knew not, turned its singing core
To words as buoyant with joy my will to do:
"In that depraved Italian land which lies
Between where Brenta and Piave rise,

And stands Rialto, is a hill that rears
To no great eminence; but down it came,
Raging, and ravening all the land, a flame
Of blackening fury. Of one seed are we.
Cunizza was I called, and here I glow
Because this star's light was mine overthrow.
But joyous am I to indulge my lot.
I fell; but in a fall that grieves me not
To backwardly regard it. Hard to thee
May seem this saying; but it will not be
If from the general herd's thou separate
Thy judgement. This most dear and shining gem
Which closest to me keeps, my heavenly friend,
Hath still a fame on earth which shall not end
Until four times again revolved shall be
The period of his first centenary.
"All men for fame contend, but which of them
A second lifetime's memory wins? How few!
This is not in the meaner thoughts of those
Whom Tagliaments and Adige enclose,
Chastised who are, taught who will not be.
But shall not soon the blood of Padua's dead
Darken the clear Bacchiglione red,
Whose necks for service are too obstinate?
"And one there is who goeth with lifted head,
Ruling where Sile and Cagnano wed,
For whose regardless feet the fatal net
Is being woven, if it be not spread.
"Loud cry the sorrows of men, but louder yet
A wail shall rise from Feltro. None shall find
A man to Malta for foul crime consigned
To match the treachery of Ferrara's priest.
God's priest to prove himself a partisan
Betraying refugees! A priest of God!
Large were the bowl would hold Ferrara's blood,
And weary who should count it, clot by clot,

That Della Tosa through that shame shall shed.
Yet even that foul deed divideth not
From daily practice of that land.
                              "Above
Are shining mirrors—thrones their earthly name—
In which reflection shows if God approve
The words I give you."
                        Here she ceased, as one
Whose mind reverted to the wheeling flame
In which again she mingled, leaving near
That other joy, of which she lately said
It had on earth a lustre. Now it shone
Like a great ruby by the sunlight smit.
For in that region those who joy of it
Glow to the measure of their ecstasy.
As those who sorrow on our earth below
Turn to the shadows of the night they know.
"God seeth all," I said, "and you in Him,
Blest spirit, see so far that naught can dim
Thy farthest vision. Never wish can be
Within thee frustrate. Wherefore then dost thou
Delay to please me with that voice which now
Delights this glowing Heaven eternally
Amidst the singing of those Holy flames
Cowled by their own six wings? Reversed with thee,
I had not waited thus to hear thee plead."
He answered: "From that ocean which contains
The earth's inhabited lands, an arm is thrust
Against the course of the advancing sun.
So far that greatest valley, water-filled,
Extends, that its Levantine eve is one
With noon above its western gates. Was I
A shoreman of those seas, in lands that lie
Between the Ebro and the Macra's stream
Which parts the Tuscan from the Genoese.
Almost alike for sunset and sunrise

The place from whence I sprang and Bougiah lies,
Which once in battle made its harbour steam
With its own blood-fall. Folco was my name,
And this bright heaven, to which by right I came,
Was then my ruler, as it owns me now.
"For never Belus' daughter, when she wronged
Both Sichaeus and Creusa, burned as I,
While youth allowed it; nor Rhodope's maid
By Phaedra's wandering son too long betrayed;
Nor he who closed his heart on Iole.
"Yet here we grieve not for remembered sin,
But smile in recollection that herein
Burned the High Value which inspired and led.
Here see we in recovered unity
The Beauty that inflamed our earthly love
Joined to the Good with which this world above
Draws back the wanderings of the world below.
"But that thou leave us well content, I show
The furthest questions which thou hast not said.
For thou the name of this near light wouldst know
Which shineth at my side as dazzling-clear
As sunlight in pure water. Know that here
Hath Rahab found her high tranquillity,
Being received this exalted sphere,
Which from your earth its shadow's point receives,
As most illustrous of your mortal dead,
Being first of all Christ's triumph rescued
To enter here among us. Well beseems
That she be shown as palm of victory
In this, or other, heaven; because that she
Joshua's first glory in the Sacred Land
Was bold to favour; which supremacy,
Scarce memorable to the Church today,
Might be eclipsed too lightly.
                      "That fair site
Which first he planted who his shoulders turned

Against his Maker—that fair city of thine
Coins the accursed golden flowers which shine
A baleful light to lead God's lambs astray.
For who should be their shepherds—what are they
But wolves at that incitement? Therefore lie
The writings of Evangelist and Divine
Unopened, while their thumb-soiled margins show
How many to the sterile pastures go
Of the Decretals, for the florins earned.
"Thereon are pope and cardinals intent,
And to the house of Christ indifferent,
Where Gabriel's wings stretched over Nazareth,
Which now the Paynims ravish. But I see
The hour when Rome's too-arrogant Vatican,
Blessed by their graves who Peter led, shall be
Released and cleansed from that adultery."

CANTO X

He, the one Value, primal, uncreate,
Ineffable, gazing on His only son
With that translucent love which constantly
They breathe through all things and all space, did form
All heaven-revolving matter and mind to be
Of such high-ordered merit that those who see
See also something of Himself therein.
Therefore, O reader, raise thine eyes with me
To where the motions of the wheels divine
Cross at their equinoctial point, and gaze
Raptured by art so heavenly-fair that He
In nightless contemplation doth survey
That which He fashioned everlastingly.
Consider how restrained obliquity
So works for earth that, were its motion more,
Changes of season were too violent;
And, were they less, how much of potency
Were dead in arid wastes. I need not say
On such a theme extended argument.
Let each man feed him where the feast is spread.
That minister of God, the regnant sun,
Who doth our earth with Heaven's live seal impress,
And measure for us time's perpetual round,
Was at that point already shown, and there
Pursued the spiral course which earlier found
Its light arise with each succeeding day.

And I was with it, though no more aware
Than one of his next moment's thought may be.
Beatrice to that goal had guided me
From good to better raised so instantly
That time of transit was not.
                Think how bright
Must be their shining in that home of light,
Who not by colour but by brilliance showed
Their presence; light in light's intensity.
Where I to call to aid all genius
The earth hath known, and all traditional art
For their interpretation, how they glowed
Would mock the attempted telling. Yet belief
May well outrun perception. Well for us
If that I tell our longing eyes shall see!
And if we fail of adequate fantasy,
What wonder is it? What to face the sun,
Is mortal vision at its best, and none
Conceives more splendour than his eyes might see.
So were we there in that Fourth Household set
Of the High Father who doth all provide;
And showeth, in itself all satisfied,
How He doth breathe through Heaven, and how beget.
Beatrice said: "Give thanks to that High Sun
In Whose great light the angels' wings are spread,
That He to this material sphere hath led
Thine upward flight."
            No mortal heart inclined
With soul more prostrate nor devout than I,
Hearing those words, myself in God to find
With will surrendered wholly. So it bent
That, for the moment, even Beatrice went
Entirely from it.
            That oblivion
She did not, though her heart perceived, resent,
But the glad laughter of her eyes outshone

In such augmented splendour that, thereon,
Was shattered in my mind its singleness
To manifold perceptions.
                              Round us bent
A glowing girdle, living, conquering,
That more than all it showed could sweetly sing,
Making itself a circling crown, and we
Its centre. Thus Latona's daughter shows
Her golden zone, with light impregnated,
When the cold air retains each shining thread.
The courts of Heaven, from whence returned am I,
Jewels of such dear value beautify
As may not be to this dark air conveyed.
They have a beauty none may bear away,
A glory not to weeping eyes displayed.
Such was their song. And though from Heaven I come
Who saw that wonder, and that song who heard,
I may not utter one revealing word.
Ye who for beauty in that mart would trade,
Wing your ascension there—or ask the dumb.
Three times, as stars around their polar star,
Those ardent suns around us whirled, but then
As dancers when the music breaks they stood,
Who pause alert to catch its notes again.
And one within itself I heard begin:
"Since in thy heart the ray of grace divine
(Whereat the Very Love is Lit to shine,
And, being lit, by loving grows therein)
Hath in thee glowed so brightly as to guide
Thy steps to climb this stair which none descends
Except for reascension, who denied
His vial's wine to sate thy thirst should be
No more in that perverse refusal free
Than water that should fail to seek the sea.
"Now wouldst thou learn the name of each bright flower
Which forms this amorous girdle, to embower

The beauty of thy lady, who doth give
Valour to thy feet to Heaven invade...I am
One who found pasture as a fortunate lamb
Of Dominic's sacred flock: he led the way
Where those might fatten well who did not stray.
And shining closest on the right to me,
Is Albert of Cologne. My master he:
I, Thomas Aquinas. If all the rest
You seek to know who form the circle blest,
Direct thine eyes the radiant wreath around,
Following my words. The next exceeding glow
Is Gratian, by his light who smileth so,
Who did so much to bring to common ground
Ecclesiastical and secular law,
That was approved in Paradise. Beyond
You see in radiance that adorns our song
That Peter who did no way boast to say
That, as the widow's mite, his toil would pay
His treasure to Holy Church. The fifth you see,
Fairest and first among us, that is he,
Solomon, of whom the doubtful world below
Thirsteth the news of his great love to know,
Of where it brought him at the last. His mind
Soared to such height; and in the depths profound
Of wisdom delved beyond comparison.
The next that shines so clearly luminous,
Is he who most the angels' ministry
Probed, and their nature: Dionysius;
And then that little laughing light beside
Is he whose Christian pleading fortified
Augustine's wisdom. Now, from light to light
Following my words, thou hast the eighth in sight,
Wherein the sainted soul rejoiceth well,
Having uncovered thy world's falsity
To all who heed him. In Cieldauro lies
His body, whence the soul outchased did rise,

Exiled and martyred, to this peaceful bliss.
"See next the flaming breath of Isidore,
And then of Bede, and Richard, who was more
Than man in contemplation. Last is he,
The circle rounded, next again to me,
Who pondered death and felt it came too slow.
It is the everlasting light of him,
Sigier, who in the *Vicus Straminis*
Syllogised truths that earned the hate of men."
He ceased; and as in God's dear Church below
His spouse salutes Him with her matin hymn,
That He may love her, and exalt her bliss,
Wherein one part will thrust and one will draw
In such sweet chiming that the spirit content
With love is overfilled, and overflows
To hear it, so I watched that glorious wheel
Resume its revolution, and rejoice
In such glad harmony of voice to voice
As may not here be told; and only be
Where joy is anchored everlastingly.

CANTO XI

Oh, blind insensate cares of mortal men!
Oh, falsehood of all arguments that turn
Eyes downward to the dust, and wings, designed
For soaring, earthward plane! One toiled to learn
Labyrinths of earthly law; and one to find
Wisdom in words for mortal cures; and one
The priesthood studied; one dominion sought
By violence, or by shrewd diplomacy;
One plunder; and the next by trafficking
To prosper; one by carnal joys was caught;
And one in ease would find tranquillity;
The while, from all inferior things made free,
Thus gloriously at Beatrice's side was I
Received and owned in Heaven.
                            When he spake,
And my round-wandering eyes the circle showed,
Pausing and turning in their harmony,
His light drew inward to itself; but glowed
A moment later with a hue more bright
The smile of its communicating light.
"As glows," he said, "the Eternal Light in me,
So gazing in that Sacred Source I see
Thy thoughts' occasions, and the way they take.
Two things you question, and would find reply,
Not in such apprehending light as I
Absorb without division of words, but so

That understanding on the road may go
Which mortal reason treads. You marked me say:
'For those who stray not should good fattening be;'
And then of Solomon: 'none saw like he.'
But here we must distinguish narrowly.
"The all-ruling Providence (Whose counsels lie
In such far depth that their profundity
Baffles the searching of created eyes)
So that the spouse of Him Who once so dear
Her wedlock purchased with His blood's red rain,
Rising responsive to His conquering cries
Should go securely to her sought delight,
Unspoiled of lowlier lovers, did ordain
A prince on either side to form her train.
One as a seraph in his ardour burned,
And one, cherubic in his wisdom, turned
A facet earthward of the light divine.
"Of both of these it were too much to tell,
For he who the one counsellor praiseth well
Speaketh of two, so like their virtues shine.
"Between Tupino and the stream that falls
Down from the blest Ubaldo's chosen hill
The slope is green a lofty mount below.
Therefrom Perugia feeleth heat or chill
Through Porta Sole; and behind it calls
Nocera for relief which doth not come
From its hard yoke, or Gualdo's. From this slope,
Where most it levels, there was born a sun
Splendid as any dawn from Ganges came;
And therefore who that lovely place shall name
Let him henceforth not Assisi say
But Orient.
    "From the dark horizon bar
To climb earth's skies he had not mounted far
Before some strengthening from his light she felt.
For in his youth he came a dame to woo

To whom most others would their doors undo,
As to the knocking of death, reluctfully.
Against his father in her cause he fought
Until he wed her in the holy court
To which he gave allegiance, while beside
His father stood surrendered. From that day
He found her every hour a closer bride
Who had been widowed such long time before
—A thousand and a hundred years and more—
Despised, obscure, her very memory dim,
Until he sought her out who sought not him.
"It had not saved her soiled repute that she
Serenely at the side of Amyclas
Had heard great Caesar's voice unmoved, though he
Shook all the world to fear. Her constancy
And courage had not saved her name, that she
Her place had taken on the cross of Christ
While Mary wept below.
     "Too covertly
I will not turn my words. Of poverty
I speak, and Francis. Lovers true were they,
As you shall hear it in plain speech. No less
Through loss of years became their tenderness,
Their joyous converse, and their amorous play.
Still in their cloudless harmony they found
Wonder and love to sacred thoughts that led,
Till others who their concord joys beheld
In such exceeding peace would find their share.
"For that the venerable Bernard shed
His hindering sandals, ran, and thought too slow
His speediest pace. Oh wealth neglected! Ground
Untilled though fertile! Now Egidius
Unsandals: now Sylvester. Following so
This bride who gives her spouse such dear delight.
"So, with his bride, the Master led the way,
Father to those the humble cord who wore.

He did not face the world abased of brow
That he was Bernardone's heir, and now
Despised and fallen to estate so low,
But kingly he disclosed to Innocent
His heart's firm purpose, and from him received
His Order's earliest license. After that,
As those poor folk became more numerous
Who on the same bare path he opened went,
Then was a second crown conferred on him,
Whose life, for earthly praise too marvellous,
In Heaven's high glory is more fitly sung,
His Order being by Honorius
Confirmed and honoured. Challenging martyrdom,
Thereafter at the Soldan's court he preached
Of Christ, and those who serve Him. Finding naught
Of fertile ground in that proud infidel court,
He stayed not vainly, but returned, and tilled
A better crop upon Italian ground.
"Then on the barren windswept rock which lies
Between the Tiber and the Arno, he
Received from Christ the ultimate sign he bore
Upon his limbs the last two years that filled
His earthly record. When that Heavenly Power,
Who for such simpleness his life had willed,
Called him to rise to the eternal dower,
Which height he had deserved by lowliness,
Then to his brethren, as his rightful heirs,
His lady he commended, that no less
Than he had served her they should serve her too,
And constant as himself her will should do,
And love her, as he loved her, faithfully.
"And after that from her dear breast his head
He lifted, rising to a realm more fit.
Yet of his earthly body still would he
Continue constant to the dame he wed,
Unclad, uncoffined, barely leaving it

To the bare earth that bore it.
                              "Think you now
What worth was in that other, who could be
Colleague to him, to steer a portward barque
Steadfast across the deep and lonely sea
To Peter's sign. Such was our patriarch.
Wherefore who followed him obediently
Is cargoed with good wares for marketing.
"But now his flock hath grown so lecherous
For other pastures than his choice supplied,
That they must wander in new glades, and thus
The further that they stray the less they bring
Of milk in udders that such journeying,
Before they reach to fold at even, dried.
"Some are there whose fair lives this charge rebut,
Still keeping closely to their Leader's side,
But little cloth it takes their cowls to cut.
"Now if my words have winged a swerveless way,
And if thou hast not failed good heed to pay,
And if thou wilt recall mine argument,
You will observe the plant they prune away;
And will perceive the hard rebuke I meant
To those rebellious sheep, when first I said:
'Good fattening is for those who do not stray.'"

CANTO XII

Even as that blest flame's last word was said,
The sacred millstone of their circle sped
Around us once again, but had not made
Its whirling; cincture once complete before
Another circle zoned it, which the more
Gave motion to its motion: to its song
A song extended: singing that so far
Excelled our own in any music played
From earthly craft's devisings tubular,
Or notes of Muse, or Syren magical,
As is original to reflected light.
As on a sunstruck mist two bows appear
When Here calls her handmaid Iris near,
Curve over curve, in colours equal-bright,
The outer from the inner born, as might
Be Echo's wandering voice, when, love-denied,
To one who would not hear she vainly cried.
—Echo consumed of love as such mists are
When the sun finds them—like the glorious bow
Which bends above the storm, and men foreknow
That flood no more the fertile earth shall mar,
As God with Noah made treaty, so did they,
The flaming sempiternal roses glow;
Their revolutions round us garlanding
In union of duality wherein
Song answered song, and flashing light to light

Was radiant.
          Then that dancing festival
Its joyous and benignant circle paused,
Accordant instant as two eyes will blink,
And came a voice from one far light that caused
My motion toward it as the needle swings
Forever constant to its calling star.
He said: "The love which causeth light in me
Its tribute to that other Leader sings
Whose servant hath exalted mine so far.
For meet it is to all eternity
That they whose war was one—his Chief and mine—
Should ever in one blended glory shine.
"For when with laggard steps the ranks of Christ
Behind his standard straggled, timorous, faint,
Ragged and few, bereft of its high-priced
Equipment, hardly to be found anew,
Its everlasting Leader, of His grace,
Not of its worth proved worthless, did review
Its dire condition, and His wisdom gave
Two champions adequate His spouse to save;
And those who heard them speak, who saw them do,
Renewed their broken ranks, and dressed again
Its front of confident war.
                    "Not far from where
Blows from the sea the gentle western air,
When with fair spring Europa's trees are glad
Returning to the summer life they had
With freshly-opening leaves: not far from where
The interminable waves on the long shore
Roll in, and break, and roll for evermore,
In from that limitless immensity
Where the sun finds no land, but meets the sea,
Lies Calahorra, fortunate, immune,
Sheltered from woe by that sufficient shield
Whereon the lion subdues and then doth yield,

Even there was born that friar faith-amorous,,
That holy athlete, pitiless to his foes,
(Which were Christ's also), but benign to those
Who followed in the faith he taught.
                          "The boon
Of living virtue was his gift so soon
That ere his birth, Heaven's meaning to express,
His pregnant mother was a prophetess;
And when the espousals at the font had been
Completed, mutual to his faith and him
In bargain of salvation, she who made
Assent on his behalf that night beheld,
In vision when the veil of sense dispelled,
The fruitful star that with his life should rise,
And through his heirs continue.
                               "So began
His life, and that his spirit should be displayed
Even in construction of his name, a power
From these high regions those who named him led
To call him Dominic, as one possessed
By Him Whom he would serve so utterly,
Being Christ-chosen for the husbandman
To prune the orchard which a negligent hour
Had left profuse and barren. Well did he
Reveal himself to be Christ's messenger,
As Christ's familiar was he shown to be.
For Christ's first counsel, which was poverty,
Was the first love his life made manifest.
And she who nursed would find him where he lay,
In wakeful gravity, as who should say:
'I see for what I came, the destined quest.'
"Oh Father, in good truth Felice named!
O Mother, Giovanna in good truth!
If these high names their first high meanings bear.
Not as men toil to Thaddeus emulate,
Or him of Ostia, for the world's reward,

But with God's manna for a nobler bait
In briefest space of diligence was he
Such able doctor of divinity
That he was fit the vineyard's rows to dress,
Which soon the vinetender's unthriftiness
Will cause to droop discoloured.
                    "To that seat,
Once more benignant to the faithful poor
—Not in itself debased, but only in him
Who sitteth on it, being degenerate—
He made petition, not for leave to skim
Rich cream from God's donations, four from eight,
Nor for preferment at a vacancy,
Nor that he might himself the tithes retain
Meant for relief of innocent poverty,
But for full license was his only plea
Against the heretic world to strive, and gain
Such harvest from the holy seed as here
In four-and-twenty plants surrounds you now.
"Then, with sound doctrine and strong purpose wed,
Armed with the apostolic right, he led,
Torrential as from some deep artery
The life-stream leaps; and in this outrage smote
The ugly stumps of heresy, fiercest where
They made most gross projection.
                         "Thence there spread
The diverse streamlets of the faith that fed
The Catholic orchard, giving leafage fair
And more abundant blossom.
                    "Such was he;
And by the chariot's one wheel wherein
The Holy Church her civil strife did win
May well be judged that other's excellence,
Of whom did Thomas with such courtesy
Inform you first. But no continuance
That chariot's circles show. Its topmost track

So long unused that no man heeds the lack
Of good wheel-surface to soft mould declined.
His should-be followers, who were vowed to tread
Their Master's footsteps, now have turned them back
So that the toe-mark in the heel you find.
And soon shall be revealed at harvesting
The fruits of evil culture, when the tare
Wails at wain-loading that it is not there.
"I say with confidence no leaf of all
Our volume now the closest search should find
To bear the boast of that obedience
Which neither runs in front nor lags behind.
Not Acquasparta nor Casale see
The light true-shining. In one place is he
Who binds too loosely, in the other, one
Who draws the cord too tightly.
     "I was named
Bonaventura—Bagnoregio
My place of dwelling—through my life I aimed
To rank the high things high, the low things low.
Illuminato and Augustine here
Beside me shine; among the first unshod
The lowly cord allowed them friends to God.
Hugh of St. Victor with these lights appear
And Peter Mangiadore. Ispano
Is here, who in twelve books taught truth below;
Nathan the seer; the metropolitan
Chrysostom; Anselm; and Donatus, who
Deigned to the art of words his hand to set;
Rabanus is here; and the Calabrian,
Joachim, shining at my side, who knew
The art of prophecy."
    To rivalling speech
I stirred at Thoma's discreet discourse,
And at his kindled courtesy, the debt
To cancel of so great a paladin;

And with approval of my purpose each
Stirred also of this goodly company.

CANTO XIII

Let him who that great sight I saw would see
Hold in firm mind this glorious imagery:
From those night-scattered stars whose rays intense
Pierce the dense air to reach our mortal sense
Most brightly, take fifteen, and add to them
The seven of that perpetual diadem
Which doth not fail by night, nor yet by day,
To circle round our heaven the wain-pole's way:
Let him with these include the further two
Which are the horn's mouth of the axle bar
Protruding from that ever-central star
Round which the circling heavens eternal wheel.
Imagine then these splendid stars displayed
In two such crowns as Ariadne made
When cold death crept around her. Let them lie
On the vast blackness of an emptied sky,
Crown within crown contained, and let them spin,
The one without following the one within,
And he shall have in vision that I relate,
The dazzle of lights, the dancing duplicate,
Of which ourselves were central.
                                  Yet more far
Beyond our use those heavenly dances are
Than would Chiana's swamp-impeded stream
Beside the eternal revolutions seem.
And so they sang, beyond our mortal wit,

Not Bacchus' praise, but far exceeding it,
Or Poean of triumph, the high unity
Of Three that are in One, and One in Three;
And how in Christ our mortal nature knew
The different unity of One in Two.
The song, and with the song the dance, were done,
And where they paused those holy Lights as one
Turned their regards in new felicity
Toward us; change with them could no way be
Disturbance of their absolute harmony.
And then that Light who had instructed me
Of him whose admirable life displayed
The poverty God approves, resumed discourse:
"Now that one sheaf is threshed, and storage made
Of its good seed, constrained by love's sweet force,
I thresh the second for thy gain. Within
Thy breast is that from which the rib was rent
Which all men seek to kiss, and all repent
The greed of those dear lips that doled them sin;
And there is that moreover into which
The lance was thrust which by its entrance gave
Full recompense for all iniquity
Past or to come; and all you are or have,
All that in Adam or in Christ became,
Was by the Ultimate Worth impregnated,
Which gave to each of these a human name.
And thinking this you wonder that I said
No other mortal to such wisdom rose
As the fifth light that now our circle knows.
"Yet heed, and you shall hear how these things be,
And look with open eyes, and you shall see
The very centre of the target struck.
"For all that dies, and all that doth not die,
Are but reflected splendour. The Most High
His own Idea through loving doth beget
Upon the material universe. That Light

Which issueth from its Source Divine, and yet
Remains unsevered therefrom, and equally
Unsevered from that Love which maketh Three,
Doth by the strength of Its benignity
Form the nine heavens, eternal, infinite,
As light refracted from its outward glow;
And through creative acts descendeth so
To those of mere contingent brevity,
Seed-born or seedless, not of one content,
For various on the wax the die's descent
Imprinteth, heavy or light, and variously
The rich bough hangs, or stand a fruitless tree;
And each man differs in his own degree
From all his fellows.
         "Were the wax exact,
And the High Virtue in Its primal act
Of one supremacy, the signet sign
Were always equal, perfect and divine.
But Nature through its myriad faults reveals
Such craft as half displays and half conceals
That which divine imagination planned
As might an artist with a trembling hand.
"Yet should the Vision Divine, the Primal Power,
Select the flawless wax, the flawless hour,
Then by warm Love were Nature perfected.
"Thus one time was mere earth made fit to fruit
In animal perfection absolute,
And then the Virgin was impregnated.
"So my conclusions with your doubt agree.
No man hath ever been and none shall be
To equal Adam or Christ. If here I stay
My course, again your wildered mind will say:
'How then was Solomon without a peer?'
But from your intellect the cloud to clear
Consider at what cause, and who was he,
Who heard the voice say: "Choose," and asked for wit,

And what the use he aimed to make of it.
"For kingly use, he made a king's request
That of all rulers he might rule the best.
To ask that wisdom to his mind be sent
Direct from Heaven by things inconsequent,
Or, at such need, of mere futility,
He did not purpose. Not so foolish he,
Nor yet so arrogant. He did not claim
To know each heavenly hierarch's rank and name;
Nor the logician's subtleties, to prove
Fault of deduction; nor that One must move
Who is Himself unmotioned; nor to try
Abstruser problems of geometry;
But for his boon he asked one excellence,
The wisdom for just rule, the prudent sense
Which so few kings possess, and all require.
"Such wisdom was his prayer; not all entire,
Which was the portion of our primal sire;
Nor that, unbounded, of our First Delight.
"So be this thought as lead, the feet to stay
From hasting to conclusion, yes, or nay,
Which doth not pause the separate cause to weigh.
Fool, and low down amongst all fools, is he
Who with too great impetuosity,
Concludes without examinations guide,
And, having chosen, through conceit and pride,
Maintains a false position. Foiled the more
Is he, than one who hath not left the shore,
Who fishes for the fact, and lacks the skill
To land it. Such in older time were these:
Meliso, Brisso, and Parmenides.
And those who stumbled with no certain will
No certain way behind them. Foolish thus
Were both Sabellius and Arius,
And others of their like whose wayward thoughts
Turned scriptural truth as polished steel distorts,

Making grotesque the seemly countenance.
"Men should not judge too swiftly, nor essay
Belief too lightly confident, as they
Who reap the harvest while the crops advance
To the green ear as yet unfilled. Hast seen
How when the winter thorn forgets its green
Harsh and malignant is the front it shows?
Yet to the summer winds it flaunts the rose.
Hast seen a ship her long lone transit steer,
Secure, fair-winded from the gentle south,
Swift and direct until her port is near,
Hopeless to founder at the harbour-mouth?
"Let not the ignorant crowd too soon declare,
Seeing one steal, and one oblation yield,
That here is hell, or God's salvation there.
Be slow to judge the event, for after all
Who fell may rise renewed, who rose may fall;
Heaven's final purpose may be long concealed."

CANTO XIV

Outward from centre to circumference
May the still water in a bowl vibrate,
Or inward to the centre, as we smite
Without it or within. This thought was mine
The transit of discourse to illustrate,
As Thomas' glorious spirit ceased, and she
Beatrice, in her turn to speak for me
Was gracious.
      "In this man a need," she said,
"Is yet unspoken, nor his thought hath made
Discovery to you or himself, to track
Another problem to its root. Reveal,
I pray thee, if those lights which now conceal
Your incorporeal spirits will remain
Around you when you resurrected gain
New visible bodies; and how, if that shall be,
So robed, you either shall be seen or see?"
As, when the festive dance will faster wheel,
And those who are and own its motions feel
The sword-play of desire in thrust and draw,
And louder-voiced and gladder-miened therefor
By their own acts augment their ecstasy,
So did those holy circles pulse and stir,
Hearing that eager heavenly voice of her,
To livelier joyance and more heavenly song.
Whoso laments that we to death belong

Knows not the nature of the eternal rain
That life refreshes to new heights of bliss.
The One, the Two, the Three, Who constant reign
In Three, in Two, in One, to all contain,
Not circumscribed but circumscribing all,
Three times by each, and in such melody,
Were hymned, that none could earn such worth but this
Were fuller payment than his claim might call.
Then did that kingly light most luminous
Within the smaller circle answer thus,
In such low voice as scarce the silence broke,
As when the Angel unto Mary spoke:
"So long as Paradise holds festival,
Waiting the resurrection hour, we shall,
To our love's measure, separately bring
This light about us for our garmenting.
As is our ardour shall its brightness be,
And as its brightness is our grace to see
Far out and high, by Heaven's benign decree.
"But when new bodies, glorious, sanctified,
Are ours, within these globes they shall not hide,
Nor shall they lose them. The new flesh will be
Dowered with continual light its God to see,
Being at last complete and excellent.
That light the vision will of God augment,
And that the ardour, and from that the ray
Will brighten everlastingly. For so,
As through the fire a flaming coal will glow
Accomplishing its visibility
Even through the flames which garb it, so shall we,
In reassertion of the flesh that lay
So long corrupt—that lieth thus today—
Being for its ultimate purpose perfected,
Rule in the light around us, which shall be
Frustrate of all frustration."
                    Answered then

From the two circles such a swift *Amen*,
And one so eager in its tone, I knew,
Even in that bliss, they thirsted to renew
Their mortal bodies, not perhaps alone
For physical joys, but that again were known
Parents, and those most dear, in days before
They thus were clothed in Sempiternal flame.
Then, as they cried, a further brilliance came,
Faint at the first, as comes at evenfall
Change in the sky, and then, uncertainty,
Expected glories, which we think we see,
But doubt our vision till the night is all.
As though a dim horizon gradual glowed
Around its full circumference, there showed
An outer, larger circle. O Divine
Spiritual Breath! These human eyes of mine
Sank baffled. Then Beatrice showed to me
Herself, in loveliness that memory
Remembers only that it may not be
In earthly memory held. Such strength she gave
I raised again mine eyes that light to brave,
And in that moment I became aware
No longer with those circling souls we were;
But with my Lady alone, the planet Mars,
That is the reddest star of all the stars,
And now seemed redder than I erst beheld,
I reached, and more exalted heights. Thereat
With all my heart I made burnt sacrifice
Of praises in the tongue that all men know.
And scarce that prayer had worded birth before
I knew it to be received in Heaven, for lo!
Such splendours opened to my sight, and so
My sight sustained them, that aloud I cried:
"Oh, God, Who in these rays art glorified!"
As, stretched from pole to pole, the Milky Way
Gleams through its studded stars, till even they,

The greatest sages, in confusion say
Its depths of light have meaning dubious,
So on the ruddy shield of Mars I saw
The venerable sign of Christian war
Set with innumerable stars, but white
With offering of its own exceeding light,
Which flashed assertion of Christ in sort wherefor
I lack device of earthly metaphor,
So that as memory turns, regarding it,
Such memory doth outreach my human wit.
But whoso for himself that Cross will bear,
And in his season shall behold it there,
May yet excuse me all I leave unsaid.
From arm to arm, from crest to base, thereon
There moved innumerable specks of light,
As the cool darkness men in daylight make
May be transthrust by one invading ray,
Wherein the motes unnumbered whirl and play.
So in continual interchange did they
Motelike their interlacing dances break
And join and alter. Crossing swift or slow,
From short to long, the specks unnumbered go.
And as sweet music turned to harmony
Of many cords of viol or harp may chime
Sweetly to one who doth not understand
The notes they render, so a strain sublime
Entranced me from those myriad notes, although
I could not follow their triumphant hymn.
Yet something of the glorious strain I knew,
For ever came the theme its accents through:
Arise and vanquish! Not these heights divine
Had brought me yet to such exceeding bliss
As now enchanted. Do I seem in this
To deprecate the joy that most was mine
Gazing on those fair eyes that gave me rest?
Do I exalt too loud inferior bliss?

No; for as yet I had not seen the best.
He whom my words confuse may think on this:
The lovelier draping gives more loveliness
To that which is most lovely. (I accuse
To make mine excusation). When I say
This bliss was greatest on mine upward way
I do not in those words contrast the sheen
Of dear sweet eyes I had not wholly seen,
And which, with each ascent from sin's alloy,
Shone with more beauty, and with holier joy.

CANTO XV

That love which the divine, benignant Will
Doth like sweet perfume through all space distil
(As will malign distils cupidity)
Silenced the music of the mighty lyre
Which the right hand of Heaven had struck to fire,
Fingering the strings of its high harmony.
How shall the prayer of human righteousness
Beat a closed gate, if these high beings agreed
Such silence merely to subserve my need?
Well may interminable grief be his
Who doth for love of mutable things digress,
And thus himself divest eternally
Of such high love as here was shown to me.
How for unlimited loss should grief be less?
For endless dole should lamentation end?
For hell's offence to cease would all offend.
As down the tranquil night's unclouded sky
A light may dart and draw the following eye,
As though some star its station changed (yet not
Leaving a vacant place among the stars,
Nor where it goes itself establishing),
So from its place upon that cross there shot
A star toward me, yet which did not leave
The cross's foot, but, gem to, scarf, thereon
Like glowing fire in alabaster shone.
Only my Master give comparison,

Telling of how Anchises found his son
In the Elysian fields, such tenderness
Was in the voice I heard: "Oh, grace divine
That thee baptizeth! Oh, descendent mine!
To whom was ever twice, as unto thee,
Heaven's gate unclosed?"
                  Such words attention drew;
Yet at my lady here I looked, and knew
A double wonder, for so bright her eyes
That here it seemed I saw profundity
Both of my grace and of my Paradise.
And then, that sight and hearing both were rapt,
The spirit's voice continued. What he said
At first I knew not. Not that he designed
To speak beyond me, but my mind, inapt
To grasp the eternal, faltered to construe
Thoughts that our mortal target overshot.
But when the bow of ardent love declined
To strike my level, these the words I knew:
"Be thine my blessings, Sacred Trinity,
Who to my seed hast shown such courtesy!"
And then: "A long-felt hunger, deep and dear,
Drawn from that sacred page which none may blot,
Had brought thee hither, and thou feedest here,
Bathed in this plenitude of light divine
From which I greet thee. That loved guide of thine
Well mayst thou thank, who gave thee wings to rise
Above the common bound of earthly skies.
"Thou deemest that to me thy thought hath way
Speechless, as from the monad rightly ray
The pentad and the hexad. Hence thy tongue
Enquires not why, these festive throngs among,
I seem most jubilant, or whom I be.
So, truly, it is. In this lucidity
We all, the greatest to the least, can see
Thy mirrored thought before it shapes in thee.

But, that love's dictates be the more obeyed,
And my foreseeing watch the more repaid,
Raise thou thy voice in Heaven, serene, secure,
Undaunted to demand decreed reply."
I met Beatrice's eyes, and they to me
Gave signal of assent, and amorously
I answered: "Equal from the glorious hour
Of thine ascension must have been in thee
Affection and perception, for the Sun
Which warms you and enlightens hath Its power
Of heat and brightness poised so equally
That in our human speech all simile
Must fail to reach it. But mortality,
For reasons which to you I need not say,
Spreads poorer wings, and less adept to soar,
Having emotion or perception more
Feathered for flight, or less. And therefore I,
Being mortal still, and having here no less
Infirmity of that unequalness,
With my heart only give thee glad reply.
"But further I entreat thee, as I may,
Live topaz that thou art, who dost begem
This sacred emblem of Christ's conquering,
That thou appease me with thine earthly name."
"Oh, leaf who from my root ancestral came,"
He answered, "thou for whose appearance here
I watched, delighting in this hour foreseen,
I give thee answer glad. Four mortal lives
Divide thee from me. He from whom derives
Thy house's name was honoured son to me.
Around the Mount a hundred years hath he
Trod the first Terrace. Very meet it is
That thy good works make sacrifice for his
Continued torment, and reduce.
                    "Oh, far
Fair vision of Florence that my mind contains!

Oh, bartered chastity for meaner gains!
Oh, sober peace of that walled girth where still
Tierce and nones from the same belfry sound!
Fair necks were there which no rich necklets wound:
Fair heads no flaunting coronets that wore.
No dames so girdled that their zones were more
To memory than themselves. No daughter's birth
Distressed the father, who with sharp dismay
Forethought of dowry, and the wasteful day,
Unmeasured in its prodigality,
Of riotous nuptials; wedding and dowry's worth
Were held in reason's bounds, nor this too soon,
Nor that too monstrous in amount. There stood
No mansions empty while their owners went
Exiled because their deeds were excellent.
No chambers yet where Sardanapalus
Luxurious ruled. Not Montemalo then
Less than Uccellatoio was contemned.
(The more the height the more the fall shall be.)
Bellincion Berti have I seen to go
Belted with leather and bone, and soberly
His dame her mirror leave with paintless face.
Of Nerlo he, and he of Vecchio,
Oft have I seen in leather jerkin clad,
And naught above it, while their dames would sit
At flax and spindle.
    "Happier days they had
Who did not doubt in their own land to die;
Who did not fear in lonely beds to lie
For France's calling of their lords; who bent
Above the cradle, soothing words to say
In that love-language parents please; who drew
Threads from the distaff while they told anew
Tales of the Trojan wars, and Filsole,
And Roman triumphs. Della Tosa then,
Or Salterello, had a marvel been

Such as Cornelia would be counted now
Or! Cincinnatus. To such life serene,
So gravely ordered, so desirable,
So stablished in its civic faith, so fair
In sweetness of its domesticity,
I passed the portal of life by Mary's grace,
In bitterness of birth-pangs called, my name
Was Cacciaguida. Your old Baptistry
So, with the boon of Christianity,
Confirmed it. Brothers of my blood were they,
Moronto and Eliseo. There came
From Pado's valley she I wed, from whom
Thy name derives. I served so valiantly
The Emperor Conrad in his wars, that he
The grace of knighthood gave. I marched with him
Against that power which holds the sacred tomb,
Our heritage, captive, to the infamy
Of those whose spiritual rule neglects
So great a purpose. In that land I fell;
Martyred by the iniquitous infidel
From the false world where hosts in bondage lie,
Not favoured by such fair release as I."

CANTO XVI

Oh, paltry honour-boast of human blood!
I will not marvel more that here below
Amid degraded passions, men should show
Pride in so poor a claim. For surely I,
Though loftier stationed in that purer sky,
Where is no baseness of desire, was stirred
To pleasure as that high descent I heard.
Yet may we price too high a failing dower,
A shrinking mantle of renown. Behold,
Time with his shears goes round it, hour by hour!
With that imperial *ye* which first was heard
In Rome's high courts, but now is least the word
That city uses, I began; whereat
Beatrice, standing some short space away,
Smiled in a manner which recalled to me
How coughed that lady who was first to hear
The fond imprudences of Guinevere.
"Ye are my father, ye exalt me so
Beyond my level, that bold heart I know
To question my desire; from streams so wide,
So various, is my kindled mind supplied
That were it sent thereby to overflow
Its natural bounds, by simple joy's excess,
I could not marvel.
        "Dear progenitor,
Tell me, I pray thee, of thine ancestry,

And in your boyhood what events prevailed
Around you in the sheep fold of St. John,
Our mutual city; how it then was hailed;
What were its loftiest seats; and who thereon
Most worthily sate."
              A living coal will glow
More brightly as the winds about it blow.
So did that topaz by my words caressed.
And as it brightened, in sweet voice and low,
In the old dialect of his time, he said:
"From that fair day which *Ave* heard, to when
My mother, sainted now, my burden cast,
Made this strong star its revolution red
Five hundred times and eighty, to renew
Its fervour where the lion is overhead
My fathers and myself in childhood knew
That street where they the yearly race who run
Reach the last Sesto. Of their periods past,
Of whom my fathers were, and whence they came,
Silence is seemlier than more to say.
But in our city in my youthful day
From bound to bound, from Mars upon the bridge
To the north wall where lies the baptistry,
There was but one man fit the sword to bear
For five now living. But what men they were!
The humblest craftsmen to the noblest line,
Each had the pure blood of the Florentine,
Not then debased from Campi's peasantry,
Nor from Certaldo, nor from Figghine.
Better by far had these as neighbours dwelt
Beside you but apart; Galluzzo still,
And Trespiano still your boundaries,
Rather than that Aguglion's hind should stench
Your streets, or he of Signa, equally
Rooting for some base chance of barratry,
"Had that high priesthood now degenerate

Been as a mother to her child benign,
Rather than Caesar's stepmother, why then,
One who is now a bartering Florentine
Had been to Simifonti sent, the where
His grandfather was once a mendicant.
"Then Montemurlo in the Contis' care
Would still remain; and still in Acone
The Cerchi dwell; and still perchance would be
In Valdigrieve, by good augury,
The Buondelmonti. All our City's woes
Spring from the mingling of its blood with those
Who crowded inward, as men gorge until
Excess of feeding brings the body's ill.
"A blind bull stumbleth to its fall, the while
A blind lamb moves uninjured. Oft we see
One sword is deadlier than five would be.
Luni regard and Urbisaglia,
High walls now ruined! Sinigaglia
Goes the same downward way: Chiusi too.
It does not seem a doubtful word or new
That noble households should themselves undo,
Since even cities like men's lives decay.
"All edifice, endeavour, enterprise,
That lifts in hope, in time's long darkness lies
A fallen loss; although its sure regress
May pass unnoted if men's lives be less.
"And as the moonled tides forevermore
Flood and lay bare, lay bare and flood, the shore,
So over Florence move the tides of time,
Ruining, exalting, base or else sublime;
So where the wonder, if the names I say
Of noble houses are no more today
High boast's occasion? I have seen decay
The Ughi; even the Catallini fall;
The Greci glory, and the Filippi,
The Alberichi, and the Ormani

Their ancient greatness lose. As proved as they,
What name hath he of Arca now? What name
He of Sannella? What of place or fame
Soldanieri or Ardinghi now,
Or the Bostichi holds?
                  "Above the gate
Which now the Cherchi with such evil weight
As may to wreckage steer the barque of state,
The Ravignani dwelt. Count Guy can claim
Descent from them, and who hath since assumed
Himself the high Bellincione's name.
"The Della Pressa then the art of rule
Had practised. Stablished in his mansion, gilt
Already was Galigaio's dagger's hilt.
"Already regnant were the arms of Vair,
And those Saachetti and Barucci bear;
Fifanti and Giuochi ruled as now;
And Galli; and that house who blush with shame
For the false measure, at a bushel's name.
"Already rooted was that stock from which
Branched the Calfucci; and in curule place
Sizii and Arrigucci. Oh, what pride
Have I seen its own fortune override
To opposite ruin! While the golden balls
Wore Florence in her haughty festivals,
Their fathers, fattening on the vacant see,
Fed grossly in the seized consistory.
"Already rose the monstrous tribe of those
Who are as dragons to their weaker foes,
But lambs to such as teeth will bare, or use
The purse's argument. From such base stock
They came that little pleasure was the word
To Ubertin Donato when he heard
Berti a bride would from his daughters give,
So that himself became their relative.
"Already Caponsacco from the rock

Of Fiesole had sought the market-place.
Already Infangato's name was high
For civic virtue, and Giuda's nigh
Of equal honour. This which next I tell
Is truth, though it be near incredible.
The ancient gate which in its time alone
Gave access to the city's central zone
Was from the Della Pera named. All they
Who that great baron's arms are bold to bear
Who still is honoured on St. Thomas' day
Do well to vaunt the worth of whose decrees
Stablished their knighthoods and their dignities;
Though he who those proud arms in gold contains
Is now the champion of the people's claims.
"Already were the Importuni known,
And the Gualterotti's worth was shown
Though still was Borgo held a quiet spot,
Neighboured by those so new it knew them not.
"The house from which your desolation came,
Buondelmonte! Through resentment just
That cut so short your joyous youth, was held
Even then in honour, and its potent name
Was it's adherents' covering shield. How ill
For thee, for all, thy failure to fulfil
Thy plighted nuptials! Light of heart had been
So many who are sunk in sadness now,
Had God's discerning mercy caused thee find
The Ema the first time you rode the bridge.
Yet was it seemly that the deed of woe
Which closed our city's peace was wrought below
The mutilated stone of Mars.
                    "But I
Saw Florence with these noble folk I named,
And others kindred, in sure peace, untorn
By faction, with no dark corruption shamed,
No cause for lamentation, not forlorn

For vengeful murders: saw its people just
And glorious. Not was then the lily on
Her crest by fractious arrogance reversed;
Nor its white ground become vermilion."

CANTO XVII

As when Phaeton came to Clymena
To end his doubting—he whose fatal zest
Still makes a father to a son's request
Slow-yielding—such was I, as both could see
Beatrice, and the holy shining star
Which from its glorious height had sunk so far
To greet me. Wherefore said she: "Loose the heat
Of yearning from thy lips, as in thy mind
It forms. It is not that thy thoughts defeat
Our swift perception; but that thou shalt find
The words that shape it."
                     "Oh, dear soil, "I said,
"Wherein my roots strike downward! Thou, so far
Exalted that, as simple problems are
Of angles to the earthly mind, so thou,
To whom all place is here, all time is now,
Canst see the coming of contingency.
Even before the unborn event may be,
Thou hast the sight to tell me! When I went
With Virgil through those pits where shades lament,
And round the Mount of Healing, everywhere
I met with warnings of great woes, to bear
My last days downward. Not my fortitude
Would prove unequal were these evils viewed
In a clear light approaching. Less the plight
Of him who sees the arrows nearing flight."

Thus spoke I, as Beatrice willed, to him,
That topas-light, whom never cloud should dim
Again from the eternal clarity.
And from unclouded vision answered he,
Not as, before the lamb of God was slain,
Dark words hid Wisdom where men searched in vain,
But in precise particularity
That love ancestral answered, with a smile
Concealing and revealing: "Left and right
A scene extends, beyond the bounded sight
One sees within the mirror. So to me
Stretches the long-dead past's immensity,
And so the future in clear sight extends.
Not therefore must you call contingency
Predestined more than is the ship that lends
Its moving shadow to the stream.
                              "Therefrom,
As cometh to the ear soft harmony
An organ utters, cometh sight to me
Of that thy later days will meet. As once
Phaedra from Athens drove Hippolytus
With spiteful perfidy, such falsehood thus
Will cut thee off from Florence. So today
He wills, he plots, he will not long delay
To act, who pondereth in that place where Christ
Is sold without cessation. First the shame
Must fall, as always, on the offended name,
But vengeance later shall the truth assert
Which arms and drives it. All you own and know
Most loved to lose as from your home you go
Shall be the first keen shaft of exile's bow.
To taste the saltness of the stranger's bread,
The hardness of the stranger's stairs to tread,
Shall vex thee next; but more thy shame shall be
In that malign and vicious company
With which thou art consorted. Ingrates all

They shall contemn thee, they revile, but yet
It is their eyes, not thine, at last shall fall;
It is their cheeks shall redden. They shall be
Self-demonstrators of their infamy,
So that thy fame shall be more surely set
Who hast for party but thyself.
       "At first,
In that great Lombard who the bird of God
Bears on the ladder, shalt thine exile find
Host and protector; to thyself inclined
In such affinity that between you two
All which are most men loth to ask or do
Shall readiest prove. Attending at his court,
One shalt thou meet so young that small report
His deeds have earned, although his warlike star
So ruled his birth that it shall lead him far
In notable deeds. Nine only times as yet
Its revolution in the eternal wheel
Hath watched his growth. But ere the Gascon guile
The noble Henry hath befooled, the seal
Of valour which he bears in deeds shall smile,
That toils shall disregard, and gold forget.
And with the years his deeds magnificent
Shall brighten to a sun beyond conceal,
So that its warmth his very foes shall feel,
And thank it. Watch his acts beneficent.
Poor men shall prosper and the haughty fall
Through him. I tell thee things thou shalt not write,
For no man would receive it." (Here he told
Incredible things I yet in silence hold,
Which those who see them shall not quite believe.)
"My son, these words the warnings heard before
Interpret truly, baring to thy sight
The snares which in short time thy steps shall grieve.
Yet be not envious of the orgulous state
Of those who overset thee. Thou shalt see

The appropriate wages of their perfidy
Before thy life's conclusion."
     When no more
He spoke, but by his glowing silence showed
That, through the warp my hands outheld, his woof
Had ceased its weaving, I in turn began,
As one who lacks clear sight his course to plan
May plead to one who loves, and hath the will
And the good wit to counsel; "Well the proof
I hear of that I dimly learned before.
And well the buffet of fate's lance I see
That spurreth on me with such certainty
A none may miss. Yet worst such impacts fall
On those the least who face them. If I lose
All else I love, the greater need is mine
To arm myself with foresight, that I choose
One path I need not for that hate resign:
The path of glorious song.
     "In that sad pit
Where wailing lasts for ever: on the Mount
From whose bright summit by my lady's eyes
I was exalted to these realms to rise:
And after, through this Heaven, from light to light,
Much learned I which, should I on earth recite,
Would be to numerous ears a bitter blend;
But if to truth I prove a timorous friend
My song may lack strong wings its course to keep
Above the waters of oblivion's deep,
To reach the ears of those, long years away,
To whom our time will seem a distant day."
The light in which my dear discovery,
Was clothed and manifest, coruscated now,
As when the sunlight counters dazzlingly
A golden mirror. "Those," he said, "who bow
Shamed heads for recollection of their own,
Or others' evil shall esteem thy song

An utterance harsh, but not for that shalt thou
Put truth aside, but in its name alone
Tell the whole vision alike of right and wrong,
Fearless of all, and stript of every lie;
And those who itch therefor may scratch the scab.
"For though thy words at first offend the tongue
With bitter flavour, yet digestion's test
Shall find them vital. Therefore sound thy cry
As winds that most upon the mountains high
Their strength exert. For this to arm thee best,
Only the souls of known or famous men
Have met thee, either in the depths of Hell,
Or round the Mount, or of the Blest who dwell
In these revolving wheels. For those thy song
Will reach hereafter would not heed events
Obscure, of those reversed in human strife,
Wholly neglected from the mouths of men.
For who will fix his faith, or shape his life
From paltry incidents or arguments?"

CANTO XVIII

That mirror of light yet in himself rejoiced
For that which to my gain his wisdom voiced,
And I yet turned it in a mind that fed
On that which proved both sweet and bitter bread,
When my dear Guide, who ever Godward led,
Charged me to change my thought. "Recall, " she said,
"That I who lead thee am to Him most dear
Who every burden casts."
                        I turned to hear
My consolation, and those sacred eyes
Such love revealed that not in anywise
Can that I saw be told. Not only so
Because my mortal speech is winged too low
Such heights of love to reach, but memory
Fails at its side, the heavenly guidance gone
That made me fit for the celestial air.
But this I know, that while that glory shone
I could not long or fear, I could not be,
Except as she controlled me. For the peace
Of Heaven illumed her, and reflectingly
Shone from her face on mine.
                           Her smiling eyes
Held me in that dear trance and then release
Alike compelled. "Behold, thy Paradise,"
She said, "belongs not in mine eyes alone;
Turn thee, and heed again."

             I looked thereon
Once more upon that flaming light, which shone
Its purpose further to discourse. It said:
"In this fifth circle of the Eternal Tree
Of which no fruit shall fail, no leaf be shed,
Which from its summit with full life is fed,
Are spirits which before to Heaven they came
Were of such eminence of earthly fame
As must the more exalt the loftiest song.
Gaze therefore on the Cross's horns, and see
How each, successive, as I speak his name,
Will flash along it, as the lightning's flame
Shows on the cloud."
                   There flashed a light along
The Cross, with which the name of Joshua
Came at one instant both to think and see;
And at the high name of the Maccabee
Another lightened, wheeling as a top
Which gladness lashes that it may not stop.
After Orlando came, and Charlemagne,
And each I followed as the eager eye
Regards across the heaven its falcon fly,
William, Rinaldo, each a following flame,
And Robert Guiscard, and Duke Godfrey came;
And numerous other lights that intershot
The glowing surface his high artistry
Chose as the worthiest ones to show to me;
Until I turned to my right side to learn
What duty might require, as word or sign
Beatrice gave, and thus her eyes I met
With joyance lit so clear and so divine
That all their previous beauty, first or late,
Could no way this high moment emulate.
And as men find delight in doing well,
And by the increase of that bliss can tell
That virtue makes advance, so there I saw

The heavenly arc in which we moved increase
Its vast magnificence of circling peace.
And by that sign our instant transit through
The space that reached a loftier realm I knew.
And as a girl's shame-reddened cheek we see.
Reverting to its cooler ivory,
So, for the red glow of the warrior star,
I saw the intense white light of Jupiter,
And in that torch the golden sparkings stir
So that in human words their motions are.
For as a flight of birds, that fields conceal
The while they feed, together rise and wheel
In ordered flight, now long, and now compact,
Above their pasture, proving in the act
Their joy of life in where and what they be,
So move those singing souls continually
Trailing to forms of L or I or D,
Chanting the words their letters shape, and then
Pausing awhile in static ecstasy.
O Goddess of the sweet Pegasean spring!
Who giveth genius the will to sing,
And with the will doth those who serve thee dower
With visions of high devise, and words of power,
By which their songs continue, and through them
May give a more enduring diadem
To cities and realms than memory else would bear,
Inform me with thyself, that I may share
This benediction. Grant me words that glow
With the high vision I saw; the power to throw
In bold relief through these poor lines the scene
That I would show to those who have not seen!
The wide white star with golden words was spread.
Thirty and five the letters there I read,
One after one, until the final M
They reached, and paused thereat. *Diligite
Justitiam* I read, and at the end:

Qui judicatis terram. On the peak
Of the last M, I saw more spirits alight
Giving the birdlike form a birdlike beak,
And singing, as I thought, the eternal right
By which all good draws Godward. There, as rise
Uncountable sparks when burning brands are smit,
Whereat the credulous stare with foolish eyes,
Drawing vain auguries therefrom, there rose
A thousand glorious sparks that there alit,
Some high, some low, as their controlling Sun
Devised it, till the patterned form entire
Was eagle, neck and head, in points of fire.
He Who in heaven that splendid sign hath prickt
Had none to teach Him. That He doth depict
Comes of Himself; as from Himself derives
The love on earth that every nest contrives.
And as I gazed on God's clear sign, I viewed
The other sparks of that beatitude
Which as with flowers the M had garlanded,
Now in more definite form their numbers spread,
So that the body and the wings became
Clear as the beak.
                O star of temperate flame!
What glorious symbol of what magnitude
Thy disc extended! By what diadem
I saw the truth in heaven thou dost engem,
That justice is divine. And hence I pray
That He Whose infinite mind did first decree
That sign, its motion and its potency,
Saw the foul smoke which doth devitalise
The ray divine; that His just wrath arise,
As once before, against the bartering
Which doth defile this temple—one not made
Of earthly stone, but blood of martyrs spilt
And miracles of God its walls have built,
Which now are shameful in their furnishing.

Oh, Heaven's warriors whom I contemplate!
For those poor sheep who move on earth astray,
Misled by pastoral example, pray!
Wars once with swords were made: by trickery
They make them now: to excommunicate
And then reopen to a golden fee.
Their coin that holy bread which God alone
Shall rule; Who will not deal his child a stone.
But thou whose hand will close the Church's gate
To make thy gain in opening—dost forget
That Paul and Peter, who the vineyard made
Which thou hast trampled for thy loathly trade,
Though for its gain they died, are regnant yet?
But thou mayst answer: "My desire is set
Alone on him whose solitary life
Went stumbling on to martyrdom; and so
Paul or the fisherman I do not know."

CANTO XIX

Gigantic in its size, with wings outspread,
That bird of God, which many souls composed,
I watched rejoice in its high harvesting.
Each of its myriad spirits ruby-red
The white star-surface in its brilliance rosed.
But that to which I now must testify
No voice hath told till now, no song did sing,
No ink indited, nor high fantasy
Fabled aforetime. This I heard and saw.
That golden beak against all natural law
Spoke *I* and *Mine*, which yet was plain to see
Multiple, whose true words were *Our* and *We*.
It said: "Because I justly ruled and well,
By service given, I here exalted dwell,
In glory absolute itself to quell
From envious longing; while on earth I leave
Such memory, even whom their subjects grieve
Revere me, though they will not emulate."
So from those duteous souls one voice arose
As many coals a single ardour glows,
To which I answered: "O perpetual flowers
Of the eternal ecstasy, who make
Your odours single! Will your justice slake
Desire which long hath held me hungering,
For which on earth there is no food to bring?
"Well know I that God's justice must appear

Mirrored in every heaven correct and clear,
But yet unmirrored its own self is here.
You know I listen with what eagerness,
You know the doubt that need no words express,
You know the unsated hunger felt so long."
As when the falcon from the hood set free
Claps its glad wings, and turns a preening head
Its plumes to sleek, that myriad entity
Woven of praises of the Will Divine,
Stirred to an outburst of triumphant song.
Then: "He whose compass masked the earth, "it said,
"And stretched its limits, and within that bound
So much made manifest, so much profound
Left beyond search, could not so hard impress
His worth upon the Universe, that less
Of virtue His remained. It left excess
Infinite and incomprehensible.
This may be seen from that first being superb
Who would not his impatient longing curb
To wait for light, by which defect he fell.
For each created being must abate
His longing to contain the increate
Infinite Wisdom; which Itself can school
To measurement by no inferior rule
Beneath Its excellence. From this we see,
The vision of finite man, which needs must be
One single light-ray from the Source of Light,
Cannot itself include the infinite,
But yet must from its Godborn nature reach
For deeper wisdom that its wit can teach.
"Reflect, how deep can any mortal eye
Pierce downward through the ocean's mystery?
How much of ocean can one eye-glance see?
It sees the shallow bottom by the shore,
But venturing outward to more depth, the more
Its sight is baffled. Yet the depth is there.

"There is no light for any soul to share
Except from that unrippled Source serene.
Besides is darkness, or the shadowy screen
Of flesh, or its corruption. Here is seen
Enough to show thee that thou canst not see.
The living justice which is hid from thee
Is there, and absolute. But thou didst say:
'A man upon the bank of Indus dwells.
How can he know of Christ whom no one tells?
He hears no speech, nor any word is writ,
Which he might welcome if he heard of it.
His words are blameless, and his thoughts are clean,
His actions, as by human reason seen,
Are sinless. Unbaptised and unconfest,
Faithless he dies. What justice may contest
For condemnation? What his fault to hold
No faith in that of which he was not told?
"You ask. But ask again. What right have you
To judge so far beyond a human view?
Your sight a span, you yet presume to say:
'That thing is wrong a thousand miles away.'
Truly, if here no Scripture ruled, were found
To human argument a marvellous ground
For long debate and subtle questioning.
But oh, gross minds! Oh, beasts terrestial!
Men went from God, the while the Primal Will
Changed not, nor from itself did deviate.
No separate good itself is increate,
But all its virtue from one source derives,
Being freely downward rayed on earth. But yet
That which is given can involve no debt."
As, when the stork its hungry brood hath fed,
It riseth on wide pinions overhead,
Circling above the nest, and those therein
Looking upward, watching what is God to them,
So did that eagle, as it ended, rise,

Broad wings of counsels multiple to spread
And so did I look upward. Song it made
Beyond my comprehension. Then it said:
"As sounds my paean to a mortal ear,
So the eternal Verdicts must appear
To those the flesh yet trammels."
                        Then it closed
Those wings that won the world to reverence Rome,
Which now the Holy Spirit so richly rosed
With flaming lives innumerable. Once more
It spake: "No spirit to this sanctity
Hath risen who was not of Christ's chivalry.
None but through faith in Him, neither before
Nor since He died upon the impious tree.
But many in the Christian lands today
Who call on Christ, shall stand more space away
At the last judgement than shall those who scant
Had thought of Him, through being ignorant.
"When the two crowds shall be disparted there,
For gain of glorious life, or else despair,
The Ethiopians shall not bear the shame,
But those who know and soiled the Christian name.
The heathen Persians shall your kings contemn
When the book opens that recordeth them.
Then shall they hear the deeds of Albert—he
Who soon shall Prague's fair land make desolate:
And he who to the Seine brings misery,
Debasing coinage, till he find his fate,
Torn by the boar's red tusk: and that fierce pride
Of Scots and English, discontent to bide
In their own lands: and that effeminate
And lust-degraded life of him of Spain:
And the like record of Bohemia's king,
Who virtue neither worked nor willed: and he
The Cripple of Jerusalem, whose gain
Of righteousness shall prove a weight too vain,

His evil deeds a thousand times as large:
And all the avarice and the villainy
Of him who hath the Isle of Fire in charge
Where once Anchises died, whose paltriness
A crabbed and stunted style would best express,
Giving small space to one whose deeds were less:
And, plain to all, the deeds exposed shall be
Of those related kings who wrought in wise
Their race and two fair crowns to bastardise:
And they of Norway and of Portugal,
And he of Rascia, whose deeds abuse
Venetian coinage, shown for what they are.
Oh, well for Hungary, if she refuse
More laceration from contending kings!
Or that the mountain barrier of Navarre
Maintain her from the woe such entering brings!
They have the example of Nicosia
And Famagosta, who lament and wail
The trampling of the beast who doth not fail
To be as ruthless as his kinsmen are."

CANTO XX

When from our hemisphere the western sun
Descends, and all the day's glad light is done,
It is not darkness that succeeds, but far
Shine out reflected glories, star by star.
This glorious image to my mind was brought
As the great bird, which was the standard wrought
For the world's empire and its leader's praise,
Closed its glad beak; for then each separate light
That formed it, each than any star more bright,
Burst into songs which then I heard; but now
Default of memory will not more allow
Of recollection. Glowing rose of love!
This only can I tell, which once above
I heard so sweetly, and so bounteous saw:
Music they were, but not as notes that blew,
But rather thoughts of God, the flute-holes through.
And after, when those lucid stones and dear,
Which the sixth heaven engemmed, had ceased to chime,
I seemed the murmuring of the stream to hear
Such as from rock to rock descendeth clear,
Fed from a generous source abundantly.
And as the sound within the lute proceeds,
Or the wind enters through the hollowed reeds,
So did anticipation end. As though
That eagle's neck were hollow, mounting so
The sound became a voice my heart was glad

To hear: and on my heart its words were writ:
"That part in me which in the mortal bird
Sees and defies the sun's high light," I heard,
"Must now be looked on, for the gems of it
Are the most choice of all the stones ashine
Which by their union make this form of mine.
"He who the midmost of their glory glows
As in the eye the central pupil shows,
Was once the singer by God's Spirit inspired,
Who led the Ark, whose glad release he choired,
From city unto city. Now he knows
How pleasing was that song to God, by this,
The place of his rewarding.
      "Of the five
Whose separate gems the eyebrow's arch contrive,
He who is nearest to the beak is he
Who to the widow consolation gave
In justice for her son. He knows how dear
The price to those who walk from Christ astray
By the sweet life God's justice grants him here,
And by the opposite of his earlier day.
"The next is he who won his death's delay
By penitent prayer. He knoweth surely now
That though tomorrows by a worthy prayer
Were gained which not in God's first purpose were,
The eternal justice untransmuted stood.
"The next in order of the arch is he
Who, with good meaning, evil fruit that bore,
Left to God's Pastor on the Tiber's shore
The rule he held, the Grecian throne to fill.
He knoweth now that that tremendous ill
Condemns him not who could it not foretry,
Though the whole world to ruin fall thereby.
"And he thou seest as the arch declines
Is William, whom his kingdom mourns—but more
That Charles and Frederick live their sighs deplore.

Now knoweth he how high doth justice bring
The place and honour of a righteous king.
"But who would credit, at an earthly guess,
The Trojan Ripheus is the fifth? No less
He knoweth now that this high eminence
He won by the celestial grace, that clear,
Beyond a mortal's sight, he probeth here;
Though even he to find its depth is blind."
As for a while the soaring lark will sing,
And then be silent in its height, as though
Content the sweetness of its song to know,
Stilled by the pleasure of remembering,
So seemed the silence of that bird divine
Which all who long therefor may gain to reach;
And though transparent in my questioning
As glass through which interior blazons shine,
Yet could I not my further words contain,
But asked abruptly: "How may such things be
As thus you tell me?"
    Then immediately
The blessed ensign, with a livening eye,
Relieved me from suspense of marvelling:
"I see that you believe the notes I sing
Because I sing them; but you see not why
These wonders are, so that, though credited,
They fail of revelation. Thus thou art
As he who knows a thing by name and sight,
But does not, till another tells aright,
Its meaning or its purpose comprehend.
"*Regnum coelorum* breaks its gates apart
Before the assault of violence. Hope alive
And love's fierce heat their conquering course contrive,
To outrage on the Heavenly Will. Not so
As man will overbear a mortal foe,
But that surrender is Its choice—to be
Frustrated by its own benignity.

"Two gems—the first and fifth—thy mind confound
That they have gained the grace of heavenly ground,
Supposing that they died in heathenry.
But this they did not. In the faith they died.
The one's clear sight foresaw Christ crucified;
The other owned Him in His later day.
"For one, through prayer's compelling might, which pled
From lips most potent at the Eternal Throne,
Came backward from the very porch of Hell
(Where none can rightly will, while there they dwell
To mortal bones resume, that he might so
Accept the Saviour he had learnt to know;
And with belief love waked, a flame intense,
That, as their second death his members felt,
Translated him to this glad eminence.
"The other, through that grace which upward wells
From springs so deep no mortal eyes can see
Even the first wave of its profundity,
Set all his heart on righteousness, until,
Being led from grace to grace, God gave him sight
Beyond the shadows of his heathen night,
So that the dawn of our redemption showed
Its light thrown backward on his miry road.
"Believing that high vision, the pagan creed
He cast aside, and raised his voice to plead
Against it with the heathen folk preverse.
Those damsels whom at the right wheel you saw
Were his three sponsors at the font—the law
Of baptism yet a thousand years away.
Predestination! In what bogs they fall
Who think they understand, yet see not all.
Oh, mortals, straitly from your judgements stay!
We who see God by Heaven's diviner ray
Know not that yet the whole elect we see.
And even this defect is dear, because
One law of God is over all His laws,

That what He willeth we alike must will."
So by this Bird of Heaven my mind was taught
To find contentment that it came so short
Of ultimate vision. As a singer's touch
The harpstrings wakens, adding more to much,
So likewise, as it spake, mine eyes had seen
Those two blest gems it named in sudden sheen
Of rapture, as two eyelids wink, assent.

CANTO XXI

Again mine eyes for my dear guidance went
To her on whom alone I now relied,
And with mine eyes my mind on her alone
Was centred wholly. But no smile replied.
"Were I to smile," with serious eyes she said,
"It were not to your gain, for you would be
To ashes turned thereby, as Semele
Died from too great a splendour.
                      "You have seen
My beauty kindled as, with straight assent,
The higher heaven we gain, and were it now
Untempered to you from a gracious brow,
Scorched would you shrink therefrom, as men may see
The lightening turn the summer greenery
To smoking ash.
                "Now have we soared to test
The seventh splendour, which beneath the breast
Of glowing Leo shows its separate star.
Look outward now, and where your glances are
Be your mind also. Mirrored in your eyes
Be all this heavenly mirror's height supplies."
Who of the wealthy pasture that my sight
Now entered knoweth, he can gauge aright,
Weighing the one side and the other side,
How fair I bartered when my heavenly guide
Mine eyes abandoned at her own command.

"In that great crystal which doth bear the name
Of the earth's ruler through that golden age
When every evil left the temperate land,
I saw a ladder. To so great a height
It rose that not my eager straining sight
Could follow, coloured like reflected gold;
And on its steps were splendours manifold,
Ascending and descending. Countless they,
Numerous as though upon those golden bars
The emptied depth of heaven had poured its stars.
As jackdaws, when the day begins to break,
Lift their chilled wings, and rise in flocks that make
Straight outward, or a wheeling course prefer,
So seemed that sparkling host, that made its flight
In groups which on their chosen steps would light.
Then one, the nighest of all, became so bright
That in my thought, as though aloud, I said:
"The love thou signest me I do perceive;
But she to whom in this strange realm I cleave,
And on whose counsel I depend for speech
Or else for silence, pauses. Therefore I
Do well my inclination to deny,
Which else would question."
                    She, who understood
The thought unspoken, answered. "Loose," she said,
"Thy keen desire." But I, in that release,
Made audible petition: "Naught in me
Is worthy thy regard. My only plea
Is the permission of this holiest one.
But for her sake this grace who granteth, say,
O Blissful life! In thy felicity
Concealed as in a garment of light, why thou
Dost come so near me, and this speech allow?
What influence to this part appointed thee?
And tell, I pray thee, why the realms below
Were loud with quiring voices, while you glow

Paradise of silence?"
                              "Mortal ears,"
He answered, "as a mortal's sight you bring
To heavenly regions. We have ceased awhile
For the same cause Beatrice did not smile.
"I settled here upon the lowliest rung
To make thee jocund with a mortal tongue,
And blissful with the light that mantles me.
It is not greater love that service gave,
For kindred fervour burns, to serve or save,
In those above us, to the most degree.
"So much their lights may tell thee, gloriously
Flashing their message of pure love. But that
Which makes us all alike most diligent
To serve that counsel which the earth controls
Selection of me made, and hither sent."
"I well believe," I answered, "how the souls
In this high court are impulsed to obey
The eternal purpose; but I see not why
You, of the sacred concourse, more than they,
Were for this deed to me predestinate."
I had not ended when that Sacred Light
Spun on itself, as with high thoughts elate,
Like to a millstone whirling rapidly.
Then from the midst its core of love replied:
"The light divine did downward concentrate,
Piercing the substance which embowels me,
So that I rose above myself to see
The Essential Source of all. But not that sight,
Nor aught made visible in its fount of light,
Gave me the answer which you seek. That soul
In Highest Heaven the most illuminate,
The Seraph who on God most ardently
Doth gaze forever, not his eyes could see
Your satisfaction. In the most abyss
Of increate light its sacred answer lies

Beyond the searching of created eyes.
"To know why that is that, or this is this,
Would bare the enigma of Reality
No mortal thought can guess. Take this report
Back to the world from which you came, that it
Presume not to pursue so great a goal.
"What are vain men to those in glory here?
Yet not to us the Eternal Thought is clear.
Shall their smoke-blinded eyes avail to see
This first immeasurable mystery?"
Informed by this repulse, I reined desire
To seemlier measure, humbly to enquire
To whom I spoke.
                He answered: "Near the land
Your fathers owned, the Italian mountains rise,
Between the one sea and the other sea
Mid-distant, to such heights the thunders sound
In valleys far beneath. One peak there is,
Catria, below whose sheltering bulk there lies
A hermitage, in which so ardently
I sought God's service that no use I found,
Come heat come cold, for aught but frugal fare.
"Good fruit to Heaven came from the cloister there
In days long ended, From its branches bare
There is not any crop to garner now,
Nor verdure to conceal its barrenness.
There Damian's Peter was I called, or else
Peter the Sinner. For a year and more
I sojourned on the Adriatic shore,
Within the cloister of Our Lady. Few
My years remaining when the call I knew
To take that hat which, as the years go by,
Passes from worse to worse recipient.
"Barefoot and lean both Paul and Cephas went,
Taking their food from any hostelry;
But modern prelates to such girth are grown

That when they journey one must move ahead
And one must hoist them upward from behind.
And as their robes about their palfreys spread
(Oh, patience which so long its time doth bide!)
Two beasts are covered by a single hide."
As thus he spoke those other flames, that shone
Upon the higher steps, began to whirl
And brighten, and descend from rung to rung.
And every motion that they made thereon
Enhanced their beauty.
Grouping round him now
A cry unto the heights of heaven they sent.
One deep articulate thunder upward went,
Beyond comparison of earth. I heard:
But, to my human hearing, naught it meant.

CANTO XXII

Distressed to stupor by that thundering cry,
I turned to my dear Comforter, as turns
A frightened child toward a parent nigh;
And as a mother, when its need she learns,
Is swift to succour, and her voice subdues
Its hurried breathing, giving confidence,
So spake she to me: "Doth your mind refuse
To know you are in Heaven? Nor argue thence
That all is holy here, and naught offence?
If lightly thus your sober sense you lose,
Think what had been if I had smiled, or they
Sung the high song that lauds their heavenly day,
Your mind disordered by a single cry!
"For, in that cry you lacked the wit to hear,
The vengeance you shall see before you die
Thundered aloft through Heaven its meaning clear.
"The sword of wrath, which smites and sundereth,
Will haste or hinder not to deal its death,
Though those whose wrong it vengeth think it slow,
And those who fear its dreadful edge to know
Think it too instant in its fall.
                    "But see
What other spirits wait illustrious,
Their earthly habitations to discuss
To your contentment. Guide thine eyes by me,
And these shall greet thee."

                              I obediently
Followed her glance, and saw a hundred spheres
Grouping themselves around us, mutually
By their exchanging rays more beautiful.
Before the lucent spheres abashed I stood,
As one who feels the urgence of desire
But for presumption lacks temerity.
Whereat the greatest and most luminous
Came forward to content me. From within,
This answer reached me: "Love's assertive fire,
Beyond thy comprehending, burns in us.
This hadst thou understood thou hadst not feared
To speak thy thought. But lest thou still be slow,
I will expose thy silent need, and show
Its answer to thee ere itself be said.
"That mount which on its slope Cassino bears
Was once with pagan temples summitted,
Where worshipped folk malign and folk misled.
I strove with those who did the Name deny
Of Him whose lowliness doth lift so high
The heads of those who own Him. Here such grace
Was granted that I cleaned that pagan place,
Routing the obscene cult's seducing power.
"These other fires were all contemplatives,
Lit from that sacred source of flame which gives
Its grace of holy fruit from holy flower.
Here is Maccarius: Romoaldus here:
Here mine are brethren who the cloister kept
Beside me. In its narrow space they slept;
Nor did they wander in their thoughts away."
And I to him: "The condescending love
You show my weakness by conversing thus,
And in those fires a guise propitious,
Tempts me to further stretch my confidence,
As the rose opens to the light above
Till every petal hath its utmost spread.

I ask thee, therefore, have I grace to see,
Bare of the hiding flame, the mystery
Which is thyself, though uncorporeal?"
"Brother " he answered me, "thy high request
Is not refused; nor is it granted now.
But when the ultimate bliss you rise to see
Is no desire but shall be granted thee
As there we also find accomplishment.
For there, entire, mature, and perfected,
Each aspiration forms its faultless flower.
"There is no past, nor any days to be,
Nor space is there, nor earth's polarity;
And as this ladder to such end aspires,
It follows that its end you may not see.
"So Jacob saw it rising endlessly,
Laden will angels. Whose the foot that tires
Lifted from earthly paths to mount it now?
Even my Order hath no lasting use
But waste of parchments; and its house of prayer
A brothel; and the hoods its brethren wear
Are sacks of meal corrupt and maggotted.
"But not so utterly the usurer's trade
Doth God displeasure as the harvest made
By greed monastic. That the Church receives
In pious offering is the equal right
Of all who truly at its altars pray;
Not for the priest who for his kindred thieves,
Or one who makes more bestial claim than they.
"The mortal flesh is so seducable
That good commencement is no warranty
That the young oak will goodly acorns bear.
Peter began his sacred ministry
With neither gold nor silver; I with prayer
And abstinence; and with humility
Saint Francis. If in turn you each regard,
The starting forth, the after-path astray,

You see the clear white turned a dingier grey.
Yet to fling Jordan back may seem more hard,
More wondrous to divide the deeper sea,
Than from such evils would God's rescue be."
At this he ceased, and those around him drew
Closer, and then, as though a whirlwind blew,
They all swept upward; and my lady dear
Impelled me to the same ascent. A sign
Was all she gave, but that sufficient cause
Moved me as never yet by Nature's laws
Men rose or fell. Believe that flight of mine
Was over ere a hand which feels the flame
Could be snatched backward. In that space I came
To reach the high sign of the Heavenly wheel
Which follows Taurus. O most glorious stars!
Impregnated with virtues luminous!
All that I am, or have of genius,
Or much or little, from your lights derives.
With you was rising, and with you would set,
That ardent heart which sires all mortal lives
When first I breathed the air of Tuscany
And then, when largesse was bestowed on me
To enter the high sphere in which you wheel,
I found your region mine. Oh, give me now,
Devoutly I entreat thee, equal power
To the hard passage that I take!
                              "So near,"
Beatrice spake, "the ultimate blessedness,
That you should seek approach with eyesight clear
And most awareness of the glories here;
And therefore, ere to more ascent we go,
I charge thee to look backward. Look below;
And see how wide a realm, and how complete,
Already have I placed beneath your feet.
For then the exultance of your heart will be
Of equal mood to meet Christ's chivalry

Triumphant in its height celestial,
When through the ether on your sight it breaks."
Then looked I downward through the seven spheres.
How mean, how paltry our proud earth appears
Seen from that height! I needs must smile to see
Its meagre aspect. O sound choice that takes
Its value at the least! How truly they
Are upright called who raise their eyes away.
I saw Latona's daughter, shining now
Without those shadows which to earth she turns,
Making me doubtful of her density;
Sustained the aspect of Hyperion's son;
And saw the daughter fair of Dione,
And Maia's son, in his vicinity
Their courses take; I saw Jove's temperate fire
Between his hot son and his chillier sire;
Observed their various orbits; all I learned,
Their size, their swiftness, and the distant vast
That parts them on their paths. And far below
The map of Earth was spread: the hills I know:
The winding rivers. All that threshing floor
For which we strive so hard, to lose at last.
So from the Eternal Twins my glance I cast
On all we had passed to that far height attain,
And turned it to her beauteous eyes again.

CANTO XXIII

Like bird at night among her leaves apart,
Brooding her nest, who feels beneath her heart
Her offspring stir, and with wide eyes and keen
Looks eastward lest the first faint sign be seen
Of dawn, while yet the dark contains from sight
The young she waits to see, her day's delight,
The bough she longs to leave, their food to bear,
(Dear, constant toil), so seemed, my Lady there
Gazed upward, rapt, erect, intent, and I
Felt as one feels who longs, he knows not why,
For that he know not.
          All my deep content,
Since to my heavenward path her hand she lent,
Passed from me; yet brief space was mine to draw
Desire's short breaths, till in midheaven I saw
A first faint light grow golden. Flower on flower
Broke sheath in heaven to form that noonlight hour.
"Lo," said she, pointing to the brightening sky,
"The squadrons of the rule of Christ draw nigh.
Himself He cometh. On his returning way
Triumph those who held His path a darker day."
And while she spake, as never words shall tell,
The brightness of that light around her fell.
Then seemed, as in clear depths of cloudless sky,
At midnight, when the rounded moon is high,
Smiles Trivia, and the eternal nymphs supply

The entire great heavens with light. For while I gazed
Toward that curtain of pure light—amazed,
Beat down, and blinded with the sight—I knew
All souls that once on earth to Christ were true
Were round Him. In uncounted hosts they came,
And formless each, one clear translucent flame.
For each soul was not, in its Master's sight,
Substantial seeming, but reflected light,
And He the Substance. Drawn across mine eyes,
A curtain were they of most living skies,
Through which I saw Him. Yet that light intense
Blinded, and as I bent, and turned me thence,
—O, Beatrice, gentle guide and dear!—
Her voice gave comfort: "That which foils thee here
Is virtue only. Naught at last conceals
Against it; here the Power of God reveals,
And here the Wisdom. Here the last New Birth
Is shown, in which Christ triumphs. For all the earth
That yearned for Heaven, and all the Heaven that bent
Toward it, separate by the gulf of sin,
Love bridges at last, and you behold herein
The bridal joys of their so long desire.
You see the path God's suffering paved with fire,
And Christ comes down it."
                          As the blackening cloud
Leans down, and in its breast the lightnings crowd,
Beyond endure, and burst in thunders free,
And none can trace them where or what they be
Thence after, so my mind, of things too great
Cumbered, gave way. It is not to relate
I lack words only. That I felt I saw
My mind refused. Again her voice. She said:
"Behold, and see me only, while I see
The banquet of the Lord of Heaven. In me
Reflected, tolerate light thine eyes may know.
I fared thereat as one whose mind doth go

Back to the threshold of a dream forgot,
And beats upon the doors, and enters not,
And may not enter, though that memory breed
Intolerable desire, and aching need.
No roadstead for a homing barque was here:
No helm for helmsman's hand who spares to steer
In dreadful, marvellous ways. But who shall weigh
The ponderous theme my feeble shoulders stay,
He shall not blame, that trembling steps and weak
Support it, stumbling to the goal I seek.
For asked she: "Wherefore are thine eyes on me
So fondly fixed, they will not lift to see
The garden in the light of Christ that grows,
And fragrant from the heart of Love's own Rose—
The Rose that from his opened veins is red,
The lilies of His life, whose odours led
The paviours that this roadway built?" And I,
As though my mistress' voice could strength supply,
Made strife against my feebler sight, and lo!
As when pure sunshine lights the bended bow
The tempest bears, or when, more like, appears
Great sunlight through a broken cloud, its spears
Shattering the gloom, and those the storm surrounds
See not the sun, but see, beyond their bounds,
A field of flowers sunlighted. So to me
Shone splendours from a place I might not see,
Shone splendours in a space I might not share,
And yet could know them. All my heart in prayer
Went upward. O, divine and kindly Power!
The name of that most fair and single flower,
The flower that morn and eve I call by name,
Bound all my mind to face that greater flame.
And as that star that earth and Heaven at one
Most laud, in glorious light before me shone,
Down from midheaven, through all its splendours, came
Separate intense, a tiny orb of flame,

That when it reached her, ringed her round complete,
A crown of light, pulsating. Song most sweet
Were discords of the storm, to that great lyre
That sounded, as their Queen was throned in fire.
O, sapphire, that the brightest heavens contain,
Central! O, song that hymns thy, deathless reign!
Clear through the breathless, waiting hosts, it said:
"I am the Angelic love. The light that led
The waiting world to God. The Uncreate Fire.
Who sheltered in her womb the World's Desire
I compass ever, height on height to tread.
O Lady, follow where thy Christ hath led!
The highest, holiest, inmost sphere shall be
Diviner, flowering all its hope in thee."
The song was ceased. The circling lights around
Returned her praise in silence sweet as sound.
And like a child its mother's breast hath fed,
Sated, that while it sinks its sleeping head,
Reaches toward her, as she rose, I saw
Those lights, constrained by Love's exceeding law,
Reach upward, lengthening, and the chant of praise,
Regina caelis rose. Not all my days
The song goes from me. Oh, what wealth was here!
Oh, gold of all our seeking, bought too dear,
Bought with one sin! Shall any weight of woe,
Labours for Christ we take, or joys forgo,
Count in this scale? Oh, great reward we see,
High gladness for good tilth and husbandry,
Abundant treasures for the tears that fell.
Are Babylon's weeping days so deep a hell?
Is Babylon's fading gold so great a lure?
Do any exiled woes so long endure?
Here, here, where Mary reigns with God's High Son,
Here is the threshold of our bliss begun.
The Eternal Gates, before the sacred Key,
Swing wide, and Death dies out in Victory.

CANTO XXIV

"O fellowship of Heaven's elect, designed
In this great Sacrament your food to find,
Given by the Lamb of God, Whose grace hath willed
That in this food are all desires fulfilled,
As by God's grace this man hath risen so far
Without the lifting of the mortal bar,
Grant that his hungered lips some crumb may taste
From the mere falling of your table's waste.
Be his strong yearning his credential here.
Let some dew fall upon him from the shower
Of which you drink so freely."
                            So she said;
And each glad spirit became a radiant sphere,
Spinning on its pole, and glowing golden-red.
Bright comets they seemed, so far their effluence flamed.
As moving wheels in clockwork harmony
Appear, the first to pause, the last to fly,
So did their dancing carol whirl, and so
Express the measures of their ecstasy.
One sphere there was who greatest beauty claimed
Beyond description in our words. He thrice
Circled Beatrice with so sweet a song
I could not hold it in my fantasy.
My pen, avoiding failure, leaps along
To possible telling. How could words create
That which, though heard, is indiscriminate

To mortal memory now? A colouring
Too violent must the earthly artist bring
To paint the intricate folds of cloth divine.
Pausing, it said: "Oh, holy sister mine,
Thy prayer, by glowing love impregnated,
Doth loose me from the circling sphere."
                                    And she:
"Oh light intense of that apostle to whom
Our Lord, before he faced and burst the tomb,
Trusted the keys of this exultant joy,
Which he to earth had taken! Test this man
On points of doctrine either light or grave
Of that high faith by which the liquid wave
Was once made solid to thy feet. You see
What sort his love, his hope, his faith may be.
Thou hast the vision which no darkness hides;
But since no citizen in this realm abides
Except he entered by true faith, it well
Becomes this man the sacred truth to tell,
And it, and our redemption, glorify."
Even as the bachelor his mind arrays,
But does not speak before the master's voice
Propounds the subject which he made his choice,
And opens it without determining,
So while she spake, with range of reason I
Prepared the faith I held to testify
To this august examiner.
                        He said:
"Good Christian, tell me, what is faith?"
                                And I
Looked to Beatrice for support; but she
An eager indication gave to me
That I should hasten in my own reply.
Thereat I answered: "May the grace whereby
There comes this high occasion to confess
To him who warward led the Christian van,

Equip my mind with wisdom, to express
The faith I hold."
So humbly, I began;
And thus continued: "As thy brother dear,
He who with thee to found the Church was sent
By Rome's conversion, with veracious pen
Wrote down for our instruction, faith must be
The substance of things hoped, the argument
Of things invisible to mortal men.
These words I take to be its quiddity."
"You answer rightly, if you rightly see
The meaning of the words, and wherefore he
First called it substance, and then argument."
And I again: "The wonders bared to me
The range of mortal eyesight doth prevent
From those below. By faith alone they see.
Thereon is hope erected. Verily
Faith is the sub-stance of that hope. And so
By faith, if faith we have, we syllogise
In sight's default. Of things unseen, he meant,
It is by faith we build our argument."
Then heard I: "If all voices loud below
Expounded teaching thus, no false surmise
Should truth confound, nor gibe of sophistry."
So spake that incandescent love, and then:
"The coin is of true weight, and right alloy,
But test we further if thy purse employ
That which thou canst so well describe."
       And I
"It is so bright, so round, the coin I bear,
That of its imprint is no line unsure."
"How gained you this dear jewel which doth bring
All virtue and all worth endurably?"
"I gained it from the parchments, Old and New,
Made fragrant from the sweet sufficient dew
The Holy Spirit poured thereon. They brought

Conviction so intense, so clear, that aught
Of demonstration seemed obtuse thereby."
Then heard I: "Wherefore didst thou count divine
Those parchments Old and New, whose words combine
To such conclusion?"
        "By the fruits they bore.
Nature no iron did ever heat, nor smote
On anvil to construct such verities."
"Yet why believe assertions so remote
From all experience of mankind? Didst note
The scripts alone themselves to verify?"
"If, "I replied, "through naught miraculous
The world were turned to Christ, its turning thus
Would be a hundred times more miracle
Than aught recorded in those scripts. For thou
Didst open that strange warfare, not as now
In glorious garb of light, but meanly clad,
Not ignorant of hunger. Thus was sown
That goodly vine which now a thorn hath grown."
As thus I said, there rose so great a cry
Triumphant through that holy court and high,
Deus laudamus, that the spheres below
Vibrated to its ecstasy. And he,
That Leader, who to trace the sacred tree
From branch to branch had drawn me, till remained
Only the outmost leaves, resumed: "You show
That Love Divine hath with thy mind conferred
To give thee wisdom, and a truthful word
Thy lips have uttered. But you have not said
What is this faith you hold, nor whence you gained
To hold it."
        "Holy Father, who dost see
Now in communion close that verity
Which when on earth thou surely didst assume,
So that thy feet were swifter to the tomb
Than those more youthful, thou wouldst have me say

The confident creed I hold, and tell the way
I came to find it; and I answer thus:
One God is my belief, eternal, sole,
By Whom this heaven, an everlasting whole,
Is impulsed with all love and all desire,
The while Himself remains unmoved, entire,
Separate. For this belief do reasons call
Both physical and metaphysical;
But the same truth I learned from Moses' lore,
And through the Prophets and Psalms. And furthermore
I learned it from the Gospels; and through you
Who wrote that which the ardent Spirit inspired.
"In the Three Persons I believe, eterne,
Of but one Essence and one Entity;
To whom both are and is, both one and three,
May be applied alike and equally.
"This is the faith I hold, profound, divine,
First learned from teachings evangelical,
Born like a spark, but like a star to shine,
A star in heaven which now transcendeth all."
"Then, as I ceased, the apostolic light,
As one whose servant makes report aright,
Three times around me circled, and three times
I heard the singing of the sacred chimes
Of benediction. So my faith he tried;
And so he blessed the words I testified.

CANTO XXV

If ever to sad hope the hour should rise
When this I write of Heaven and all between,
Which through long years of toil hath made me lean,
Should be of potency to overset
The bitter verdict which forbids me yet
The sheepfold where I slept, as a lamb lies
Foe to the wolves which are its natural foes,
Then with changed voice and different fleece from those
With which I fled shall I return to wear
The poet's chaplet at the font which there
Once saw my baptism. There the Faith I knew
Which introduces souls to God, wherethrough
I came where Peter now encircled me.
But moved another light from out the sphere
Where grouped the vicars whom Christ bid declare
The tale of His salvation. "Look how near,"
My lady charged me with glad eyes aware,
"He cometh, for whose sake Galicia's shrine
The pilgrims throng in that far world of thine."
As at the mating time an amorous dove
Circles and coos and bows around its love,
So these high captains of our faith I saw
In rapturous greetings join, that praised the feast
Which by the boon of Heaven their joys increast.
These greetings done, they faced me silently,
Yet in such radiance that mine eyes abashed

Sank down before them. But she spoke for me:
"O lustrous life, who told in sacred writ
The largesse of our court, make hope to sound,
I pray thee, in this height. On earthly ground
Thou didst personify the lure of it,
When Jesus on the Mount was glorified."
Then in response that second splendour cried:
"Lift up thy head, and with assurance gaze!
For naught can to the middle earth belong
But it must ripen when it feels our rays."
Thereat I raised mine eyes grown confident
Toward the heights of Heaven, that sank before,
And he continued: "Since our King hath meant
That with His nobles, in His sacred Hall,
Thou shalt confer before thy death befall,
That thou hereafter shalt these sights recall,
And strengthen in thyself and those who heed
The hope that doth all earthly hope exceed,
Say now what this hope is, and how to thee
It flowered, and by what course it came to be."
But she so dear, who with such tenderness
Had nursed my wings for this high flight, my word
Prevented with her own: "There is not one
Of all the militant church on earth more rich
In that high virtue; scrolled upon the Sun
Which guides the armies of God, that truth is clear,
Therefore was he allowed to enter here,
To come from Egypt to Jerusalem,
His years of mortal warfare yet undone.
"But those two further points I leave, that he
May answer, not as aught unknown to thee
Exposing in his words, but that he bear
This record back to earth, and tell to them
Who have the grace to heed it. This will be
Not difficult to him, nor boastfully
Will he have need to answer. May God's grace

Now make him equal to his need."
                          And I,
So heartened, as an eager pupil will,
In haste by answering to reveal the skill
His Master tests, made confident reply:
"Hope is the sure and fixed expectancy
Of glory waiting in the days to be,
Born of God's grace, and merit precedent.
From many stars hath come this light to me,
But first I learned it from the voice of him
Who sang supremely of the Lord supreme.
For said the Psalmist: 'Let them hope in thee
To whom Thy name is known;' and what could dim
That name to faith like mine? And next I read
The words of thine Epistle. Filled thereby,
Such hope could overflow, and fructify
In weaker hearts than mine."
                          As this I said,
From out the living centre of that flame,
A flash intense and swift as lightning came,
From which there followed: "That high hope I had
Which flameth still, which naught on earth forbad
Even to the field I left, the palm I won,
Willeth that with thee should my flame be one,
Who in thy warfare hast the same delight;
And further is my wish that thou shouldst show
What promised pleasure in thy hope doth glow."
And I to him: "The scriptures, old and new,
The symbol showed, and from that sign I knew
The essential fact the friends of God declared.
For, as Isaiah said, the robes are shared
By those God blesses in their earthly years,
When to the sweetness of this life they rise.
And in thy brother's vision more appears
The evident truth in clearer exercise,
When in his revelation he declares

The two white robes the saint in glory wears."
I scarce had ended when the loftier height
Rang over us, aloud with Heaven's delight.
Sperent in te the exultant clarions cried,
And all the carols to this shout replied.
Then from among them flashed so strong, so white
A glory, that the world would know no night
In winter days, were such a crystal set
In Cancer, to redeem the low sun's debt.
As some glad virgin, with no thought beside
The joy and honour of her friend the bride,
Steps out and dances, to herself display
In all her beauty, so this splendour came,
Joining the others in their zone, and they
Wheeled in the dance of love's intensest flame.
And as the bride they praise may stand content,
Watchful of all, unmotioned, reticent,
So stood my lady, 'See,' she said, 'the man
Who on the bosom of our Pelican
Once rested; who was chosen from the Cross
Our Lady's comfort in her mortal loss.'
As one who gazes for the sun's eclipse
Till blindness cheats him, so my dazzled sight
Surrendered to the overwhelming light
Of this last glory; but its voice I heard:
"Why art thou dazed by that which is not here?
My body rose not from its earthly bier.
Nor shall it, till the tale of God's elect
Be totalled. In all heaven there are but two
Who the two robes may wear till God renew
Creation from the dust. Take back this word
To those who doubt it."
                      As he spoke, the rest
Their motions and their singing ceased, as when,
For weariness of toil, or perilous shores,
The whistle shrills above the straining oars.

Then I Beatrice sought, my sight to test,
And could not see her, though she stood to me
So nigh, and in high Heaven's felicity.

CANTO XXVI

As I stood blinded thus, a voice there came
Directed to me from the blissfull flame
My sight that conquered: "Till again you see,
Recovering that you have consumed on me,
The compensation of discourse is thine.
Say therefore on what thoughts thy mind is set;
And doubt not that thy sight is flawless yet.
It is defeated, but it is not dead.
For she who upward to these heights hath led
Hath in her eyes the power that one time lay
In Ananias' hand."
                "Let what come may,"
I answered, "in this realm where all is good;
For what God willeth, it is all I would.
And at what time she choose, or soon or late,
Be these eyes opened which were once the gate
Through which she entered with the kindling fire
Of mine unquenched insatiable desire.
The good which gives these lofty heavens content
Is first and final in love's argument;
Of all the scriptures the intent is this,
Either implied or taught with emphasis."
The voice which had my blindness comforted
Urged me again toward discourse. It said:
"You needs must shake a finer sieve than that.
Say why this targe your bow was bended at."

I answered: "Dictates of philosophy,
And old traditions of authority,
Showed me at first the good I loved to see.
For good, being seen, because it is the good,
Wakes love. The more that it be understood
The more it gains by its own excellence;
And therefore will the mind itself direct
Toward that essence which such virtue is
That nothing else of any worth can be,
Except it have its virtue drawn from thence.
"This truth is to my mind interpreted
By him who doth the primal loves detect;
It is interpreted as certainly
By Him Whose voice *ego ostendam* said,
Omne bonum tibi; interpreted
No less by thee, whose writing didst proclaim
The interior secrets of this holy place,
As none besides revealed it."
            Then I heard:
"The reason for your love which first you tell,
By intellect and by authority
Confirmed, is primal, and you answer well.
But tell me if no other cords there be
That draw thee Godward: if no other teeth
Which close and drag thee to the love divine?"
Not hidden from me was the high design
Through which Christ's eagle sought my faith to see,
Whereat I answered: "Yea, such grips are mine.
All powers of love that move the heart combine
To hold me in that close captivity.
The existence of the world, the mystery
Of mine own being, and most powerfully
The death He suffered that I should not die,
The hope His followers have to live thereby
(Which hope is mine), these various cords supply
A net to draw me from the darker sea

To the safe shore of right love's verity.
Each leaf of the fair garden God creates
As it with Love the Gardener cultivates,
So must I love it to the like degree."
I scarce had ceased before the sweetest strain
Mine ears had heard through Heaven was sung; and she,
My lady, *Holy, Holy, Holy,* sang,
Joining the acclamations; and thereat,
As when a strong light strikes on slumbering eyes,
So that the spirit within must wake and rise
To meet it as it penetrates, but still
Confused and blinded by the light, until
Adjustment and reflection gain control,
So did Beatrice to mine eyes restore
The sight I squandered, with one glance's ray,
Which had not, though a thousand miles away,
Unequal to that rescue been; and more
Of sight she gave me than I lost before.
And as my vanquished sight returned to me
I saw four glories where had been but three.
And of this wonder, as though stupified,
I dumbly made demand, and she replied:
"Within that splendour, holding converse high
With his own Maker, is the ancestor
Of all mankind."
               As, when the wind comes by,
We watch the bending of a downward bough,
So was my soul bowed down in wonder now;
And, as the bough resumes its previous place,
So to that glory did I lift my face
Restored by eagerness to speak: "O thou,
Who wast not seed, but as a fruit mature
Came to the garden of God! To every bride
Father, and father to the spouse she takes,
Be thou complaisant to mine eagerness
Which asks no less because no sound it makes,

Knowing I have no need to thought express
To win thy comprehending, and that less
Than any speed of speech is thought's delay."
As, when a cloth above a beast is spread,
Itself concealing, if it lift its head
The moving cloth its motion indicates,
So that first soul within its glory stirred,
To prove its pleasure at my speechless word.
It breathed: "Though nothing of thy thought was said,
Yet clearer to thy secret thirst I read
Than thou couldst state thy greatest certainty,
Because the truth, as every truth, I see
In that great Mirror which is sight to me,
Which mirrors all, but is not equally
Mirrored by aught beneath it. You would ask
How long the time since God uplifted me
To that fair garde in which, so long a stair
To mount, thy lady did thyself prepare;
And for how long mine eyes that pleasure knew;
And of my fall the explanation true;
And what the language that I used and made.
"Believe, my son, the bitter price I paid
Was not because I plucked so fair a tree,
But that God's order I contemned thereby,
Four thousand and three hundred years and two
I dwelt in that sad region whence for you
Your lady Virgil sent. Nine hundred year
And thirty, earlier, had I watched the sun
Encircling heaven before my days were done.
Long ere the sons of Nimrod toiled to rear
The tower that should remain unsummitted
The language that I made was lost and dead;
For of all human works will naught endure.
That men will always fashion speech is sure,
And sure that men will change it diversely,
As diverse minds determine.

"Ere I went
To face the grief infernal, That which sent
All good to earth, Which all good radiates
In the high Heaven, was Yah; but after that
El; but such change no change did signify.
For as a leaf will flourish, and then die,
And freshly, as another year goes by,
Another leaf is green, so change is sure
In human use. For human works to dure
That were the only change that will not be.
"On the fair mount of Paradise I stayed,
With life dishonoured and yet purified,
No longer than from sunrise until when
The sixth hour cometh to the world, and then
I mounted, and I here in Heaven abide."

CANTO XXVII

"Glory unto the Father, and the Son,
And to the Holy Spirit." So loud the cry,
So sweet, which through all Paradise rose, that I
Stood as intoxicated by delight.
Not only hearing was possessed: my sight
Alike was ravished. O the rapture there!
The gladness inconceivable! The life
Compact of joyful peace and peaceful joy!
The wealth so absolute beyond compare
No longing can be felt, no jealousy
Were possible sin, if sin were possible.
Glowed the four lights with yet intenser glare
The while they faced me, and I saw that he
With whom I first had converse changed his hue,
As Jupiter and Mars two birds should be,
And change their plumage. That control which gave
Order and function to the blest had stilled
The heavenly choirs, as that red splendour spoke:
"Thou shouldst not marvel that I change my hue,
For these who stand beside will change it too,
Hearing my condemnation. He on earth
Who hath usurped my seat—my sacred seat—
Who hath my seat dishonoured—which is now
In God's sight vacant—he my sepulchre
Hath made a privy whence is drained to hell
The blood and filth obscene which pleases well

The arch apostate from this Heaven who fell."
As intervening clouds at dawn or eve
Redden as they obstruct new day begun,
Or close the path of the retreating sun,
So did I see all heaven a crimson shame
While this was uttered. As a faultless dame
May be confused by some immodesty
She doth not share but is constrained to see,
So did Beatrice's aspect change. I thought:
Such was the eclipse which shamed the Heavenly Court
When on the cross the Prince of Glory died.
But he who spake proceeded, not the tide
Of indignation changing more his due
Than it his voice transmuted: "Christ His bride
Was not established by my blood, or that
Of Linus or of Cletus, that she should
Be used for gathering of ignoble gold.
It was for gain of this fair Heaven that they
Sixtus, Calixtus, Pius, Urban shed
Their blood in deaths that many a tear foretold.
"We had no thought that half Christ's flock should stay
At our right hand, and half be forced astray
To leftward; nor the sacred keys I held
In trust for the Eternal be the flag
Flown over fields of death, where Christians slay
Christians baptised but excommunicate;
Nor that my head upon the seal should be
Of purchased pardons, which mendacity
And greed, in bold defiance of God, create.
"Oft at such deeds doth indignation stir
And redden me as you now behold. They howl
Rapacious through the pastures, pastor-clad.
Rescue of God! Can even God defer
The vengeance that would save us? Cahorsines
And Gascons banquet on our blood. Oh dawn
That looked so fair! We had not thoughts such scenes

Its noon should darken. But my hope remains
That that high Providence which loosed the chains
Of Rome by the good sword of Scipio
Will bring deliverance soon. And thou, my son,
Whose witness on the earth is not yet done,
Be not thou silent among men. To them
Bear witness of these things you hear from me.
For condemnation of what I condemn
You need not fear to utter."
                    As we see
The frozen vapours in white flakes to fall
When the Sun feels the Goat's extended horn,
So through the ether rose, like flakes of fire,
Those lights triumphant. Not could sight aspire
So high to follow. When my lady saw
Mine eyes absolved of straining: "Look," she said,
"Look downward. See how far thine arc hath sped."
Then downward at her word I looked. From when
I looked before, through the first clime had we
Moved from mid-arc to reach its end. Below
Was Cadiz, and beyond, the shoreless sea
On which Ulysses ventured foolishly.
And on the other hand the distant shore
From which the bull the raped Europa bore.
My sight on earth's extended threshing-floor
Had that way further pierced, except the sun
Had travelled forward, by a Sign and more
Advanced beyond us.
                    But my subject mind,
(Which gladliest its loveborn food would find
In ever gazing on my lady's eyes,
That all which nature made, or art designed
Of beauty through the sight the mind to win,
All loveliness of flesh, to art akin,
With all that pictures excellence combined,
Were naught to her one smile), from that far sight

Returned my gaze.
                The power those eyes possessed
Drew me in swift ascent from Leda's nest
To those most lofty heavens where all is one;
So that I say no more 'was here the sun',
Nor 'here some constellation known to men'.
All in that realm of live intensity
Was like and likeless to my gaze. But then
She saw my longing, and her smile on me
Was as though God within that smile could be,
As thus she answered: "All reality
Round its fixed centre moves; but in this height
Where God is all the love and all the light,
Where is no otherwhere, no where can be.
Love graspeth all in one including zone
Of mystery only to its Maker known.
"What language can define infinity?
Five is the half of ten, but that to see
The limit of the ten must first be seen.
Here is no limit of space; and naught hath been,
Nor will be, ended or commenced. Behold
The roots of Time's full-leaved but fading Tree!
Oh transient greed of earth for transient gold!
Which downward draws the eyes which else were raised
To this fair height where none hath vainly gazed.
Truly the will of men is fair in bud,
But round his roots the filth's continuous flood
Makes the fruit putrid at the ripening hour.
"Innocence and faith are in the opening flower,
But, with the beard's growth, virtues fade away,
And in the loss of childhood lost are they.
How many children fast who, breaking free,
Will eat all meats all months in like degree?
How many to their mothers cling and learn,
Give love for love, who, as the seasons turn,
Will count impatient to her burial day?

Thus is the sun's fair daughter, virgin-white
At dawn, befouled before the fall of night.
And lest thou wonder that the years should bring
From such glad dawn so dark an evening,
Reflect that none bears rule on earth—or they
Lead only who can only lead astray.
"But ere that slight defect of count which brings
The winter months more near to future springs
Shall bloom the January rose, on high
Through this great Heaven shall rise the conquering cry
That peals arrival of the fated hour
When every sail shall spread, and every prow
Swing, as the helm bids, where the poop is now;
And fruit be set from every opening flower."

CANTO XXVIII

When I had heard that truth so contrary
To what we suffer now, or what we see,
From her who to my mind brings Paradise,
Then, as a man may in a mirror view
A taper move behind him, ere his eyes
Have seen it, or his thought have known it there,
And as he then might turn to learn the more
Of what is meant, or who the taper bore,
And see it as the mirror showed, as like
As words to wedded music, so to me
A wonder came that yet I did not see.
For in those eyes which love had made the net
To be my captor, such a spark was set
And when I turned to know its origin,
And on mine own that Glory glanced which all
Who raise true eyes to Heaven behold therein,
A point I saw which not can thought recall,
Nor words be found for that intensity
From which my glance rebuffed and blinded fell.
In the whole heaven there is no star so small
But this keen point of light were smaller far
Than a moon's smallness to that smallest star;
And at such distance as a halo spreads
When mists are densest round its source of light
There spun a circle of fire so furiously
That not the coursing of the swiftest sphere

Could emulate its motion. Circling near
I saw a second outer band of fire
That in its zone enclosed the first entire,
Round that a third, and yet a fourth, and yet
Three more, the seventh of so wide a bound
That were full circle made of Iris' bow
It would not round that outmost circle go.
Yet was an eighth, and yet a ninth beyond,
Each of more moderate speed as its degree
Was further from that core of unity.
Of these, the inmost had the brightest flame,
Because, as I surmised, it closest came
To that most pure and vital spark within.
My lady saw my questioning doubt, and said:
"From that bright point doth all that is begin,
And all concludes. The inmost circle see
How swift it whirls! Love from that pivot inspires
Its furious speed, but the remoter fires
With lessening ardour reaches, that they spin
Outward from zone to zone more moderately."
To which I answered: "That is plain to see,
And such the evident cause. But contrary
Moves the material universe, for there
The outmost circles have the best compare,
And take the swiftest motions. If I knew
Why the reflection doth its source deny,
Then were my reason satisfied; but I
On this angelic miracle of light
Gaze vainly, asking that which mortal sight
Is futile to discover."
          "If the knot
Thy fingers fumble, therefore wonder not.
Hard are its strands because no loosening pull
Hath ever touched it till this hour. But heed
The thing I tell thee with attention full,
And on it work thy wit. As more or less

Of virtue hold they is the spaciousness
Of all material spheres. High excellence
High bliss must bear, and must itself express
More amply, being in its constituents
Alike, and differing only in degree.
Therefore the one which more desire contents,
With deepest wisdom and with liveliest love,
Must be that one, the smaller heavens above,
Which all includeth and encircleth all.
"And if thy thought avoid this test of space,
And think of virtue only, then you see
That they are equal in their own degree—
The outmost sphere: the inmost zone of light.
"Greater to more, or smaller into less,
No different are they, equal to express
The grading of the Intelligences, as they
Intensest shine, or pour their virtues wide."
As thus my lady to my doubt replied
In luminous words, my mind became as clear
As, when the winds of earth's wide hemisphere
Blow gently, laugh the skies serene, and show
The beauties of the landscape stretched below.
Clear as a star in heaven the truth she set,
And, as she ceased her words, each coronet
Shot forth innumerable lights, as shoot
Sparks from the bubbling iron; and every one
Danced in its circle at its circle's speed,
Numerous to any mortal count defy,
As we the chessboard's squares may multiply.
From choir to choir those flying motes I heard
Hosanna sound, one sole exultant word
Raised to that point round which they pivoted,
Which bindeth and shall ever bind them there,
The placeless, whereless, but eternal *where*
Which is their place for ever.
                              Then she said,

Observing mine unspoken eagerness:
"The inmost circles have revealed to thee
The Seraphim and Cerubim. So fast
They spin around that central source that they
Shall share its verity the most they may.
And as their vision is sublime, so far
They gain their purpose.
                    "Those their course beside,
The loves that round the next swift circle ride,
Are named the Throne, because they brought to be
Completion of the primal ternary.
And you should know that their delightings are
According as their sights can penetrate
The truth which quietens every intellect.
From which we can perceive the blissful state
Is founded on the sight of God direct,
From which love followeth in its course. The sight
Is merit in itself, which grace begets,
And the desire for holiness; and so
From grade to grade doth the sweet process go.
"The second ternary which flowereth thus
In this eternal spring, where never night
Sees Aries trample, doth perpetually
Unite in its hosannas, which it sets
In three accordant strains of melody,
As the three orders of its gladness are.
For here are three ranks of divinity;
Thus ordered—Dominations, Virtues, Powers.
"The third, last ternary consists of these:
First Principalities, Archangels next,
And, last and outmost, Angels flame and sing.
All these gaze upward, being so drawn, and draw
From downward with a might as victoring.
"These are the orders Dionysius saw,
With such keen vision yearning to the height
Of Heaven, that each he named, as now to sight

They spin before thee. Gregory made surmise
That differed, so that when he opened eyes
In this serenity, he smiled to see
His earthly error.
              "Marvel not too much
That mortal mind had pierced such mystery.
One, as you read, was snatched to Heaven, and he
Disclosed it, with much else these circles see."

CANTO XXIX

As when in Heaven Latona's children twain
The opposite horizons occupy,
One by the Ram, one by the Scales possessed,
And one must sink from sight, and one must gain
Solitary dominion in the sky,
So long as in a balanced poise they lie
Ere either wholly to one hemisphere
Belong, Beatrice with a silent smile
Observed my longing, gazing fixedly
On that bright point which held infinity.
Whereon she spoke: "I will not ask to hear
The question that thou wouldst, for I have seen,
Even there where all things are and naught hath been
When all things are and therefore naught shall be,
Thy mind's full nakedness, and so to thee
I do not ask, but tell.
         "No aim of gain
Unto Himself, which gain could no way be,
Moved the Creator, where eternally
Beyond the intrusion of Time He dwells, beyond
The comprehension of a mortal brain,
To form His creatures; but the will to see
His glory shine in a reflected glow
Which of itself *I am* could testify.
Love was the impulse, that more loves should show
The eternal love that formed them. Do not dream

That once, as slumbering in Himself, He lay.
Creation is an ever-moving stream,
Sourceless and mouthless. Neither start nor stay
Belonged it ever. Matter and form apart
And mingled came, as from a three-stringed bow
Three perfect arrows. As in crystal clear,
Or glass, or amber, will a light enclose
Throughout and instant, so the threefold rays
Instant and absolute and everywhere
Their work accomplished. How could be *before*
Which is of Time, before Time was? Or how
After of Time, if Time should be no more?
"Order with substance one creation shared.
Highest of all pure Actuality;
Lowest was pure Potentiality;
And midmost Power, with Actuality
Inseparably united. Jerome said,
Long ages ere aught else creation knew
The angels only were. But had he read
With clearer eyes what all who search may do
In scriptures by the Spirit of God inspired
He had not blundered thus. And something here
Might reason urge. For why should angels be
Long ages while their functions useless were,
Being formed to serve a world which was not there?
"Now the beginnings to thy mind are clear.
You know the order of the Loves that here
Exult in their swift ecstasy, and so
Three flames of yearning cease as these you know.
Know further that no man should count a score
In so short time as on Creation's shore
A part of these bright angels headlong fell
Beneath the level of Earth. But these remained
In harmony divine, and so began
Their dancing circles, where, being self-enchained
By the excesses of their own delight,

They whirl for ever. He the fall who led
Was lost because his evil pride outran
The eminence God bestowed. For which you saw
How hardly just inexorable law
Had thrust him underneath the whole world's weight.
"But those who revel here were swift to see
The Source from which they came, and modestly
To own and praise It; in response whereto
Their vision clearer, more exalted grew,
As their own merit was by grace replied
With light that by reflection multiplied,
Until they burned God's service to fulfil
By their own separate and established will.
For be not dubious of the fact that they
Who to God's grace their hearts wide open lay
Have merit in that receptivity.
"Now, if your mind have garnered all I say,
By contemplation mightst thou comprehend
Much more of this consistory. But since
Your schoolmen in their lecture-rooms contend
That the angelic nature understands—
Remembers—wills—I will some further light
Contribute to their dubious sophistry.
"These creatures never, since the joyful day
When first they waked to God, have turned their sight
From Him, wherein are all things evident,
Past or to come. Their eyes can never see
A thing unseen before; nor memory
Diverted thence, a previous sight recall,
Always and presently aware of all.
"But earthly men although unsleeping dream,
Talking such things as may or may not seem
Truth to the talker. More the fault and shame
Of those grown subtle in deliberate lies;
But few on one clear path philosophise,
Impulsed by love of notoriety,

And seeking theories which will bring such fame
As schoolmen covet. Yet this mimicry
Of wisdom less of indignation wakes
In Heaven than when the very script divine
Is tortured from its sense, or thrust aside,
By those who think not how its seed was spread
With tears and toil and blood of martyrs shed,
Or how well-pleasing are the steps that tread
Humbly the path long-trodden.
                       "Each to shine
In his own light designeth, and contrives
His own inventions, and the pulpits sound
With vain debating, while the evangel lies
Untaught, neglected. One man says the moon
Covered the sun when its Creator died,
Another that the sun its light denied
To all men at that hour the whole world round,
So that the Indian and the Spaniard knew
An equal darkness to the impious Jew.
The Lapos and the Bindos are not more
In Florence streets, than in its pulpits breed
Such worthless fables; and the sheep who need
A fairer pasture on mere wind are fed,
Excuseless that they ask no better bread.
"Christ did not to his first disciples say:
Go forth, and chatter trifles, but He showed
A true foundation, and a heavenly road.
The evangel was their lance on every field,
The evangel ever was their certain shield,
The evangel was their battlecry. But now
They preach with jests and mimic posturing,
And if some jape a gust of laughter bring
The hood blows outward with the wind it makes,
And all is approbation. Could men see
The bird that backward in that cowl abides,
Then might they guage the brand of pardoning

To which they trust; but such false confidence
Hath grown on earth that any vain pretence
Is taken, proofless of its worth. Thereby
The swine are fattened of St Anthony;
And men, more swinish in their sense than they,
For such false coins as have no imprint pay.
"But since we have digressed sufficiently,
Turn back thine eyes the present scene to see,
So that we journey by the time allowed.
These angels you behold so myriad are
That neither thought nor speech can reach so far
As could their numbers understand or tell;
For that which was revealed by Daniel
Sought no determinate number to express,
But rather that their hosts were numberless.
And as their numbers, so the primal light
On each doth with a different glory smite;
And as doth each its diverse light receive,
So variously it doth itself conceive
The love which it reciprocates thereto.
Behold the infinite Height and Breadth! No two
In all that host identical ardour burn.
Each to one mirrored Love doth love return
Diversely from its own diverted view."

CANTO XXX

As when, with noon six thousand miles way,
Thick darkness on the couch of earth may lie,
But light is visible to the loftier sky,
So that the stars their growing doubt betray,
Until one here, one there, will lose its power
To light our floor, and with the mounting hour,
When the sun's loveliest attendant shows
Above the coming of dawn, the fair light goes
From the mid-depth of heaven, to us profound,
Of one star and another star, until
The brightest takes invisibility,
So did those high triumphant rings of light
Fade in succession from my doubtful sight,
Ceasing from their appearance, one by one,
To include the All-Including, till remained
Naught visible but that point too blinding-bright
For mortal eyes to meet it. Hindered thus,
And by my love compelled, I sought the sun
Which never sets to me. If all before
That I of her have writ were joined to raise
One sweet impassioned melody of praise,
It were not equal. Beauty here was more
Than mortal speech attempteth. Only He
Who made it, surely to the full degree
Could joy in His creation. Here I plead
Defeat in most extremity, to exceed

All past frustrations of the sons of song.
No poet ever of high comedy
Or tragic fall, so far was overcome
By sword thrust of a theme more great than he.
I think of that I saw, and am but dumb.
The intensest sunlight was her smile to me,
As when it falls on eyes least adequate
To face so great a glory. From that day
When first I met her till this hour I tell,
My song hath never ceased nor turned away
From worshipping her beauty. But this height
Hath foiled me. Nevermore my pen will write
The memory of that loveliness. No more
My song will follow on her beauty's track.
All those who seek the highest are beaten back
At last by this default of words. I leave
This theme to a more triumphant trumpet-call
Than mine, which falters as its long attempt
Draws near to its conclusion.
     This she said,
With swift and confident words, and gesture sure:
"Behold, from out the Heaven of greatest space
Passed have we to the sphere where light is all;
Light intellectual by pervading Love
Impregnated: pure love of holiness
Impregnated with bliss, which bliss transcends
All separate sweetness. Here your eyes shall see
The twofold chivalry of Paradise;
And those who from an earthly conflict rise
In the same aspect as their forms shall be
Before the throne of judgement."
       Suddenly
As lightning blinds, a living light around
So swathed me that no further use I found
For thwarted sight, of that sole light aware.
But hearing had not left me.

All who share
The Heaven which Love to its own quietude
Subdues, doth this baptism of light include
Into Itself, the taper to dispose
To take the flame. As these words came to me,
I felt within myself surmounting power
That conquered all I had been, and therewith
Was sight new-given of such supremacy
That it all brightness might confront, although
Most absolute in essence. There I saw
Light like a river in its molten glow
That golden flowed between two banks aflower
With spring's fresh miracle. From out the stream
Came leaping sparks that in the blossoms fed,
Rubies in cups of sunlight. Each would seem
To sate itself with fragrance, and return
As others outward leaped that joy to learn.
"The more," she said—oh, ever sun to me!—
"The strong desire doth urge and burn in thee
To understand the marvels thou dost see,
The more I pleasure; but I tell no more
Till thou art further fitted to explore
These heavenly wonders. Thou must drink for that;
For all thou canst perceive doth no way be.
The stream itself, the leaping Topaz lights,
The banks, delicious in their first delights,
Are but dim preludes to reality.—
Not that these glories in themselves repel,
But that thy sight is not accustomed well
To this superb occasion."
                    Never child
By too-long sleeping from its food beguiled
Runs to the milk as then I bent in haste
The marvel of that flowing gold to taste.
O splendour of God! Through which, in Heaven's height,
I saw the triumph of that true realm aright,

Grant me the words a wondrous sight to show!
For as when folk unmask at carnival
Fair faces, when mine eyelids met the flow,
It changed its length to roundness, and for all
The previous beauty of the sparks and flowers,
Lo, the two courts of Heaven were manifest!
But where are words their wonder to declare?
A light transcending every light is there
By which His creatures their Creator see,
Where only in that sight their peace may be.
So large circumference this light doth bind
That, should it test its use, the sun would find
It wore too loose a cincture. All its rays
Strike upward to the Primal Motion, thence
Reflected round and downward.
                            As a hill
Images itself in some clear lake, as though
Upon its own rich verdancy to gaze,
So in that light, around that eminence,
Round and around in thousand ranks I saw
The conquering saints of God. And if so low,
So large the light, the concourse, nearly viewed,
Judge what must be the outmost amplitude
Of the wide petals of that golden rose.
But not the great breadth nor the ample height
Could give denial to mine eager sight
Of the full sweep of that ranged ecstasy.
For, where God is, nor near nor far can be,
Nor Nature's laws have any meaning there.
Within the yellow of the eternal rose
Beatrice drew me, while its petals spread
Wide open to that sun which round it shed
An everlasting spring, the while its praise
Continual perfume gave. "Behold," she said,
"The mighty concourse to your sight unclose
Of all the white-robed victors! See what girth

Our citadel requires! Behold the thrones
So filled that few there are who fight on earth
And have not claimed their places. . . . That which draws
Thine eyes, being vacant, where a crown is set
Above it, waiteth him whose righteous cause
Shall strive to bring relief to Italy,
The imperial Henry, who his seat shall fill,
Before yourself at this high bridal feast
Shall sup among us. Vain that strife shall be,
For, blinded by its rash cupidity,
Your country, like a starving child, doth still
Chase its own hope of life, its nurse, away.
And he who holds the sacred seat shall ply
Friendship at once and secret enmity
Until God thrust him, in short space, to lie
With Simon Magus—forcing lowlier yet
Him of Anagna for his earthly debt."

CANTO XXXI

Like a white rose with open heart to see
Were ranged the ranks of Christ's great chivalry,
Which with His blood, a sacred spouse, He won;
And those angelic birds who, while they fly,
Do sing His glory Whom continually
They serve, and by that service magnify,
Being of it enamoured as they are,
Like swarming bees of which each one doth sink
Within some flower's bright petals, there to drink,
And then fly back to where the toil it bore
Is turned to sweetness in the general store,
Did each for ministry himself embower
Within the petals of that spacious flower;
And then ascend, to that fair realm regain
Where doth the constant fount of love remain.
Their faces were of lively flame: alight
Their wings with lustrous gold: the rest so white
That dull in contrast were the whitest snow.
And as within the flower they ministered
With fanning wings the ranks of saints along,
Passion they gave and peace alike to know;
For in the bliss of that most holy state
Passion is peace, and peace is passionate.
Nor did the multitude that came and fled
Obstruct the vision of the light above,
Nor mar its penetration. Potency

There is not in the universe to stay
That light from those found worthy. All the love
And all the light in this sweet realm are one,
Most joyous in their high security,
Where all of worth to enter, old and new,
Find love and vision are a single word.
O triune light, which in that single star
Doth flash to their content so wondrously,
Look down, the storm that sweeps our world to see!
If the barbarians, from cold lands afar
Which watch the wheeling course of Helice
Yearning for ever in her son's pursuit,
Were stupified by wonder, led to gaze
On Rome's high ramparts, where the Lateran
Towered highest, transcending all the works of man,
Should I not stoop to more extreme amaze
Who here from mortal to immortal came?
From time to face eternity? From those
With whom I mixed in Florence, to consort
With sanity and justice? With this weight
Of wonder and of strangeness bowed, and moved
With joy beyond conceiving, asked I naught
Awhile but silence, thus to contemplate
Confronting marvel.
          As the pilgrim stands
Within the temple that he vowed to see,
Gaining new life therefrom, while memory
Already casts its eyes about, to store
For after-telling, so mine eyes I led
Through the live light among those myriad bands,
Now up, now down, and now their lines along.
Faces I saw that dear love lit, made fair
Both by the sacred light around them shed,
And by the smiles that they returned thereto;
And in their attitude mine eyes could view
Honour, and grace, and dignity.

                          As yet
Attention on no single point had set,
But the whole scope of Paradise had filled
Both eyes and mind; and now I turned to get
The interpretations that I sought, from her
Who had so constantly my craving stilled,
Not doubting aught. But what I thought to see
I saw not. At my side an Elder stood,
Gloriously apparelled as those victors are.
With kindly-smiling eyes he looked on me,
As might a father in benignity,
But in quick doubt I queried: *"Where is she?"*
To which he answered: "Here Beatrice willed
My presence, thy desire to culminate.
But look thou to the circle third below
The ultimate honour, and thine eyes shall know
Her merited throne." And making no reply
I raised mine eyes and saw her.
                          Seated high,
The living everlasting light divine
Crowning her brows with its reflected rays,
I saw her, far from any reach of mine.
Far as from darkness of the deepest sea
The thunders of the utmost heaven may be,
I saw her inaccessible. Not for that
I saw less clearly. Naught could intervene
In that pure space where all alike is seen.
"O Lady," to the distant height I cried,
"In whom my hope is yet unsatisfied—
Who to redeem me, when from grace I fell,
Hast left thy footprints in the halls of hell—
Through whom the bounty and the potency
Of these high regions have been shown to me,
Led by thy virtue in its excellence—
Thou who hast drawn me from where slaves belong
To view the freedom of the sacred throng,

By all the cords thou hast! I pray thee now
Still magnify thy liberality,
So that my soul at death's release may be
Well pleasing to thee."
                So I prayed, and she,
Despite the distance, met mine eyes with hers,
Smiling upon me. Then her glance withdrew,
Again that fount of joyous light to view.
Then spoke the holy Elder: "Prayer and love
Assigned thee to me, that thou mightst complete
A perfect progress. Cast thine eyes about
This light-drenched pleasance, gathering power to meet
The extreme brilliance of its source above;
The Queen of Heaven at last thine eyes shalt see.
For her I burn with love, and therefore she
Her grace will grant. Her faithful Bernard I."
As the Croatian pilgrim stands at gaze
While our Veronica is shown, amaze
And reverence for that ancient miracle
Trancing his eyes, while in his thoughts he says;
"My Master, Jesus, very God, was this
Truly thine aspect to the eyes of men?"
Motionless till it be withdrawn, so now
I gazed on him who gained that love to live,
By beauty of a life contemplative.
But his rebuke aroused me. "Son," he said,
"Favoured of Heaven, too long you leave unknown
This joyous region, while its base alone
Your eyes regard. Look up! Look up! to see
The higher circles to the most remote.
The enthroned Queen of Heaven your goal should be,
To whom this realm is subject and devote."
I raised mine eyes. The oriental sky
As dawn approaches, doth indemnify
Its claim to fairness, while the contrary
West is horizoned in a paler light.

So saw I, as along a mountain height
Seen from the vale below, the boundary
Of the top petals of that open rose
Showed at one point superior. As when
The chariot-pole Phaeton could not guide
Is driving upward, near to sight, the glow
Precedes it, while the skies on either side
Are gold less glorious, did that circle show,
Amidst its general oriflamme of peace,
One point of all most radiant, equally
Fading on either hand. And over it
A thousand angels making festival
Hovered and sang and sported; every one
Distinct in art and function, separately
A thought of God created.
                         Words are none
For what I now beheld. If wealth of speech
Were mine to equal all I dream, I yet
Could no way to that height of memory reach.
Conception will nor compass nor forget
The smallest part of that deliciousness
For which the victor saints of Heaven are glad.
Saint Bernard saw the keen delight I had
To gaze upon the source which filled his joy,
Whereon his own devotion turned his eyes
Back to the same direction, so that I
Mine ardour from his own did fortify.

CANTO XXXII

His love still centred on his most delight,
With holy words that saint contemplative
Became my teacher. "She, so beauteous,
Who ever sits at Mary's feet," he said,
"Is our first parent, who the wound exposed
Which Mary by divine conception closed.
In the third rank are those of next degree,
Rachel beside Beatrice: after these,
Sarah, Rebecca, Judith, and beyond
The Moabite maid who was the ancestress
Of him who sinned and sang, and in the stress
Of penitence *Misereri mei* cried."
Petal by petal, rank by rank, he told
That concourse of illustrious names of old,
Half-circling down the rose's rounded cup,
Until the seventh zone he reached. "From them,
Even as before, go down unnumbered names,
But ancient all, a tale of Hebrew dames
And others who, before Christ's victory,
Looked forward, and believed the light to be.
"For this side of the rose are only they,
But on the other—note the cleft between—
Are those who loved the Christ their eyes had seen,
Or looked with faith upon a backward day.
"Therefore is every petal filled complete
On the one side, but many a vacant seat

Is on the other, waiting those who yet
Shall rise triumphant.
        "O'er one side is set
The high seat of the Queen of Heaven alone;
But o'er the other, on an equal throne,
Sits high and sole that John the holiness
Of desert life who dured, and martyrdom;
And who, for his delivering Lord to come,
Waited two years within the gates of Hell.
"Seated beneath him Francis, Benedict,
Augustus see; and how, from row to row,
The conquering Christian saints are ranked below.
Behold the prescience and the high design
Of the forecasting providence divine!
Equal at last the tale of seats shall be
Of those who on a risen Christ relied.
And where the rose is cleft on either side,
Concourse from concourse clearly to divide,
Sit they who come to God unmerited
Either by deeds or faith, their lives too soon
Expiring. Heaven allows this ample boon
On sure conditions. Note the infancy
That still their voices and their faces tell.
Now thou art troubled, and a doubt too hard
Thou wilt not speak! But thou shalt heed me well,
And loose that subtle knot's complexity.
"Within the limits of this perfect garde
Naught may intrude by casuality,
More than may grief or thirst or hunger be
Within its realm for ever. All you see
Is here established by divine decree,
Close-ordered as the finger fits the ring.
Wherefore these folk whom grace to life doth bring
After so short an earthly journeying
Are not accepted without sound pretence
Of active or of passive excellence.

"The King Who formed this realm, which hath no night,
Of every love compact, and all delight,
So that no thought should dare to add to this
The vain conception of more perfect bliss,
Hath mind created in His Own glad sight
Endowed with many graves diversely;
And this high court of bliss which here you see
Doth vindicate His wisdom wondrously.
This truth explicit is in scripture shown,
As when those twins unborn, within the womb,
In anger differed. Different worths assume
As different aspects here, enchapleted
To equal their prenatal grace: as keen
As turn they to the light, the light responds.
"In the first ages innocence alone
Secured salvation to the child of those
Who were themselves devout. A later day
Allowed male children such release if they
Were circumcised and sinless. After that
The period of full grace full rite required
Of Christian baptism, that the innocent wings
Should gather power to soar.
                    "But turn thy mind
The ultimate goal of thy long quest to find.
Fix on the fairest in this sacred place
Thine eyes full adoration: hers the face
Which of all faces is most like to His
Who was her mortal Son. Its radiance
Alone can fit thee Christ Himself to see."
I looked and saw. No earlier marvellings
Through all upward mine upward course were like to this:
No other semblance seemed to God so nigh.
Those angels who frequent the loftiest sky
Cast rapture round her, while that minister
Who first had said the joyous words to her
Ave Maria, spread his wings to bow

In reverence toward her as he sang them now.
His song the holy rose from every side
Returned; and as the choiring bliss replied,
On every face upraised, serene before,
There came a new contentment.
                              "Father, who,
Leaving the seat of thine eternal due,
Hast condescended to me, wilt thou tell
That angel's name who loves his Queen so well
That, as he gazes on her eyes, he seems
Aflame with adoration?"
                         He who drew
Beauty from Mary as the morning dew
Shines from the sunlight, answered: "Equally
Sweetness and triumph meet in him, for he
Brought down the palm to Mary, when the Son
To bear our burden was Himself undone.
Praise without envy unto God we give
That his joys are to ours superlative.
"But turn thine eyes to follow, while I tell
Of the high paladins of Heaven, who dwell
In this august dominion. Those whose seats
Are highest, either side our Queen most high,
And so most blissful, being to her most nigh,
Are as two roots from which one single rose
To this supreme exultant beauty grows.
"He on her left hand, of our race the first,
Is he whose rebel hand audacious durst
Pluck the sweet fruit which had such bitter taste
To all men after. On the right is he
To whom Christ gave the keys of liberty
To enter this fair rose; and next beside
The seer of Patmos who, before he died,
Beheld the tribulations of the bride
Who with the nails and with the Lance was won.
"And seated by that other, he who led

The folk who were with meals of manna fed,
Thankless, inconstant, mutinous. The next
To Peter seated, Anna, keeps her eyes
Fixed on her daughter in such tranced wise
That even *Hosanna* she omits to sing.
And next beyond the greatest ancestor
Sits Lucia, she who, when thine eyes, perplext
By earthly travail, lifted not to see
This periled heritage, thy lady roused
To be thy rescue.
                    "But the moments flee.
Short is thy time allowed. The tailor cuts
According to the cloth. Thy glances now
Lift to the Ultimate Love! Endeavouring
As far as may be possible to thee
To penetrate its incomparable light.
"But since weak pinions from so great a height
May flutter backward, let us pause to call
For aid so powerful that thou shalt not fall.
Heed thou my prayer for grace not impotent,
Following me with a single mind intent,
That not words only, but the heart be there."
So speaking, he began this holy prayer.

CANTO XXXIII

"Virgin and Mother, Daughter of thy Son,
Humblest and highest of our mortal race,
In whom was Hell's dark counsel first fordone,
In whom high God took being without disgrace,
So did our nature gain in nobleness
From thine incarnate purity: through whom
Love warmed the eternal peace within thy womb
To bear the flower we now unfolded see!
All love is sphered in thee, all loveliness
In thy bright torch; and those who wait below
In thee the living spring of hope shall know.
Lady, such greatness and such worth is thine
That any who without thine aid would shine
Would wings contemn the while he seeks to fly.
Not only those who on thy grace rely
Are fenced about by thy benignity,
But oft thy succour doth the prayer precede.
"In thee is pity for the human need,
In thee is tenderness to intercede,
In thee is largesse of that excellence
Which doth include all valours of soul and sense
Wherein thou art supreme of all create.
"Lady, there is one here who comes equipped
With earthly soilure. One whose feet have dipped
In Hell's deep cesspool. One whose eyes have viewed
Each tribulation, each beatitude,

Which grades the glories of the upward way.
Now doth he for this greatest mercy pray,
That he may lift his mortal eyes to know
The ultimate bliss. I never burned to plead
For deeper vision for myself with more
Intensity than now I speak his need.
But do thou yet my prayers intensify!
I pray thee, add thy prayers, of potency
More than are mine, that he be purified
From every stain of his mortality,
The supreme ultimate Light unveiled to see.
"And further, Queen, I for his rescue pray
That thou, whom all things must on earth obey,
To serve thee thy desires, shalt grant him this:
That not the vision of so great a bliss
Shall lose its power upon him. Grant that he
All human impulse may in future rein
To heavenly purpose. See Beatrice, how
She doth with folded hands entreat thee now,
And the ranked saints alike my prayer sustain."
Those eyes, to which one time, with childhood's love,
God had looked upward, now looked down to see
Her suppliant, with a glance that tenderly
Expressed her gladness at devotion's prayer.
Then to the eternal light that showed above
She raised them. None create, it well may be,
So deeply into that strong light shall see.
Thereat I knew the culmination nigh
Of that long pilgrimage, and reverently
I stilled mine aspirations, all my mind
Emptying, the fullness of High God to find.
Saint Bernard signed me now that Light to know,
But I already of myself was so
As he would have me. Eyes unvanquished now
Lifted and saw. With deepening gaze I knew
The simply, utterly, entirely True.

But what I saw therein no words could tell,
No human memory from God's citadel
Retire with plunder of its wondrous store.
As he who dreamed, and can recall no more,
Nor that from his encumbered mind dismiss,
So toiled am I. I know no more than this:
I dreamed. I waked. I know the sweetness yet,
Though the deep source my yearning thoughts forget.
Where is the snow that faced the mounting sun?
What search shall find it? When the winds were done,
Where had the leaves of Sybil wisdom blown?
Yet something, O Thou Light Supreme, Alone,
Transcendent of all mortal search! Allow
To recollection. Something grant me now,
Though but one spark, that I once more may see!
And power of utterance, that their eyes may glean
Some splendour backward brought who have not seen!
Surely it must be to Thy praise that I
Bring something back to earth, some memory
To tell in human speech inadequate
That inexpressible glory! This I know:
Had mine eyes wavered from that sacred glow
I had been irretrievably lost. Therefore,
Aware of peril, did I strive the more
The weight of infinite value to sustain.
O grace abundant, which supplied my sight
With strength to face the everlasting Light,
To comprehend and be consumed therein;
Which gave me power in that profundity
All things created through all space to see
Gathered by Love to form a single gain,
Like pages scattered, lost, but once akin,
Regathered, in one ordered book to be.
All incident, all accident, and all
The crossing chances which to men befall,
All varying substance and perverse event,

Were here made perfect, in one brightness blent.
This I believe with mortal eyes I saw,
For as I ponder that supernal law
And as I now declare it, ecstasy
Floods through me, with no other cause to be.
Not five and twenty centuries have hid
The Argo's launching, since the distant day
When its broad shadow on the waters slid,
Amazing Neptune, as that moment did,
Separating itself from mine unequal mind.
Intent, oblivious, rapt, I gazed to find
My heart enkindled from a source made blind
To recollection. At that fount divine
Shall no man drink so deep a draught as mine
And thirst for coolness of a different spring.
For all wills seek the good, and everything
Of good, of every kind, is there complete
Which men may otherwise defective meet,
Partial at best, there perfected. My speech
Strives, but no further to its goal may reach
Than might an infant's tongue, the milk that feels
Drawn from its mother, as it now reveals
The Ultimate Wonder. Not that more or less
Was in that Light, its essence to express,
Than one unvaried semblance. Yet therein,
As my sight strengthened to explore, I viewed
Three shining circles of one magnitude,
But diverse in their coloured beauty. Two
Were Iris unto Iris. But the third
Was from the Others breathed, an effluent fire;
From each an equal radiance. Oh, how crude,
How slow to soar is any human word,
To that which recollection holds! And how
Doth memory strain and fail to picture now
That depth of increate Light! O Light divine,
Who art Thyself Thine own abiding-place!

Who all dost comprehend, and all embrace;
Who by Thyself must comprehended be,
But by none other: Who Thyself dost see,
And inwardly upon Thyself dost shine,
And in that contemplation take delight,
Love on Itself reflecting!
     As I gazed,
It seemed that form was on that painted Light
Pictured in human semblance. There I raised
Eyes tranced and raptured by that wondrous sight.
As the geometer the circle strives
In vain to measure, thinking uselessly
For that he lacks, which yet he knows must be,
The evading principle, so now was I.
How did the image with the circles blend?
How were they separate? This to comprehend
I strove, as wingless worms might strive to fly.
Yet for one flashing instant even this
Was granted. Vain, recoiled, remembered bliss!
My mind sank backward on itself, too far
Lifted to there establish. But no less
Desire and resolution formed to press
My purpose, like an equal-rolling wheel,
This marvelled revelation to express
In words that naught pervert, and naught conceal,
Urged by that Love by Whom all creatures are;
Who guides the sun, and every following star.

ABOUT THE AUTHOR

SYDNEY FOWLER WRIGHT (1874-1965) penned over seventy volumes of science fiction, fantasy, classic mysteries, historical novels, poetry, and non-fiction, many of them being published by the Borgo Press imprint of Wildside Press. Please visit his website at:

www.sfw.org

www.ingramcontent.com/pod-product-compliance
Lightning Source LLC
LaVergne TN
LVHW040116080426
835507LV00039B/388